# HERSTORY

### By: DR. ELMIRA P. DAVIS

**IF YOU DON'T LEARN FROM HERSTORY, YOU'RE DESTINED TO REPEAT IT!**

Trafford
PUBLISHING

Unless otherwise indicated, Scripture quotations are from the King James Version of the Bible.

Order this book online at www.trafford.com/07-1432
or email orders@trafford.com

Most Trafford titles are also available at major online book retailers.

© Copyright 2007 Dr. Elmira P. Davis.

All rights reserved. No part of this publication may be reproduced, stored in a retrieval system, or transmitted, in any form or by any means, electronic, mechanical, photocopying, recording, or otherwise, without the written prior permission of the author.

Note for Librarians: A cataloguing record for this book is available from Library and Archives Canada at www.collectionscanada.ca/amicus/index-e.html

Printed in Victoria, BC, Canada.

ISBN: 978-1-4251-3650-5

*We at Trafford believe that it is the responsibility of us all, as both individuals and corporations, to make choices that are environmentally and socially sound. You, in turn, are supporting this responsible conduct each time you purchase a Trafford book, or make use of our publishing services. To find out how you are helping, please visit www.trafford.com/responsiblepublishing.html*

*Our mission is to efficiently provide the world's finest, most comprehensive book publishing service, enabling every author to experience success. To find out how to publish your book, your way, and have it available worldwide, visit us online at www.trafford.com/10510*

**Trafford** PUBLISHING www.trafford.com

**North America & international**
toll-free: 1 888 232 4444 (USA & Canada)
phone: 250 383 6864 ♦ fax: 250 383 6804 ♦ email: info@trafford.com

**The United Kingdom & Europe**
phone: +44 (0)1865 722 113 ♦ local rate: 0845 230 9601
facsimile: +44 (0)1865 722 868 ♦ email: info.uk@trafford.com

10 9 8 7 6 5 4 3

# CONTENTS

| | |
|---|---|
| **DEDICATION** | 5 |
| **ACKNOWLEDGEMENTS** | 6 |
| **ABOUT THE AUTHOR** | 8 |
| **FOREWORD** | 10 |
| **INTRODUCTION** | 14 |
| **CHAPTER 1   ABIGAIL**<br>PERSEVERANCE (run and don't look back) | 23 |
| **CHAPTER 2   ANNA**<br>FOCUS (mine eyes have seen the glory) | 37 |
| **CHAPTER 3   DEBORAH**<br>COURAGE (what's your assignment?) | 53 |
| **CHAPTER 4   ESTHER**<br>BOLDNESS (oh) | 63 |
| **CHAPTER 5   FIVE WISE VIRGINS**<br>WISDOM (running on f-u-m-e-s) | 73 |
| **CHAPTER 6   HANNAH**<br>HOPE (what is your due date?) | 83 |
| **CHAPTER 7   JOB'S WIFE**<br>ANGER (let the lord build your house) | 95 |

**CHAPTER 8   JABEZ'S MOTHER**                    *109*
    DESPAIR (plan 'b')

**CHAPTER 9   SAMARITAN WOMAN**                *117*
    ATONEMENT (looking for love in all the wrong places)

**CHAPTER 10  SAPPHIRA**                            *127*
    DISHONESTY (lay it on the line)

## CHARACTER TRAITS IN ABC ORDER:

    ANGER                              *139*
    ASSURANCE / FOCUS                  *140*
    ATONEMENT                          *142*
    BOLDNESS                           *144*
    COURAGE                            *146*
    DESPAIR                            *148*
    DISHONESTY                         *150*
    HOPE                               *151*
    PERSEVERANCE                       *152*
    WISDOM                             *153*

**ENDORSEMENTS**                                   *155*

# **DEDICATION**

I would like to dedicate this, my first book, to my mother, Laura Pollocks, my greatest inspiration down through the years. Even though I was the youngest of seven children, she refused to spoil me and encouraged me to be accountable for my actions.

She used a lot of **mama-nyms** (Wise Sayings) while I was growing up and I find myself using the same ones when speaking to my own daughters.

She is a strong woman with a good sense of humor, a strong faith in God and an undying love for her family and friends.

I'm thankful for a praying mother!

# ACKNOWLEDGEMENTS

A special thanks to these wonderful people who, in some way, contributed to the completion and success of this, my first book.

To God the Father, His son Jesus and the precious Holy Spirit for your awesome presence in my life, and for the gift to minister Your engrafted Word to Your people through teaching, impartation, singing, and example.

I am thankful for my lovely daughters, Krystal and Kadriane, who work beside me in the ministry and give me unconditional love.

I honor my loving and supportive sisters and brothers, Nettie, Jessie, Thomas (T.C.), Lonnie, Mattie and Mittie. Thanks for sharing your lives and love with me. Special thanks to Mattie and Mittie for being my greatest cheerleaders and for allowing me to talk for hours and hours about my God-given vision for this book. Thanks Mittie for double-checking my editing efforts.

Special thanks to my brother, Lonnie Pollocks, who demonstrated unconditional love by post-poning college to get a job to support our family during some very rough times.

Thank you, to the faithful members of our church, New Destiny Church of Christ Written In Heaven, for your prayers and for covering your pastor.

I give special honor to my spiritual bloodline, anointed vessels who have sowed into my life and supported my ministry in so many ways: Pastor Eula Mae Nelson, and the late Bishop Nathaniel Pollock, National Mother Clara James, Dr. Mildred Foster, Pastor Bertha Brooks, the late State Mother Alice Jackson, District Mother Ethel Mae Skipper, Diocese Mother Maylis Harrison, District Mother Cleo Baker, Dr. Abe Johnson, Jr., Pastor Mary Holloman, Pastor Sarah Battles, Pastor Dorothy Lee, Pastor Rosalind Tomkins-Whiteside, Pastor Becky Dickey, Pastor Nathan & Mary Wachob, Mrs. Cheryl Huffstickler, Minister Beverly Burnough, Mrs. Emily Lou Clay, Evangelist Jacqueline Williams, Mrs. Delores Hudson, my former church family at Tabernacle Church of Christ Written In Heaven and a special thanks to the global family of brothers and sisters in Christ.

Thanks to the many students that I've taught, their wonderful parents, and the wonderful faculty and staff at the wonderful learning institutions where I've taught. You continue to show me love and respect as we partner together to help our students achieve their personal best.

Thank you to all of my family, friends, extended family, and supporters for being part of my testimony.

# ABOUT THE AUTHOR

**Pastor Elmira P. Davis** received the baptism of the Holy Spirit in Rochester, New York and has served in many capacities in the ministry for over 25 years. She is a visionary leader with a God-inspired awareness of what people really need to be complete in Him.

She is the Senior Pastor of New Destiny Church of Christ Written In Heaven in Tallahassee, Florida. She is conference host and the founder of the Annual Women of Destiny Conference held each year in February. She is the creator of the **"LET GO AND GO ON"** workshop for women and encourages them to let go of excess spiritual baggage and step into their God-given destiny. She is a sought-after preacher, speaker and workshop presenter for district, state and national conferences and church events. Two recent discussion manuals that she presented at the national level include "Church Etiquette and Pulpit Protocol" and "Avoiding and Dealing With Offenses in The Church".

Pastor Davis is a graduate of Florida State University with degrees in Audiology and Speech Pathology. She is employed by the Leon County Schools and was nominated for the Glenn-Howell Distinguished Minority Educator Award in 1994 and again in 2004 when she represented Leon County as one of five finalists. She has taught Public Speaking and Interpersonal Communication courses at Tallahassee Community College and is nationally certified and licensed to practice privately as a Speech Pathologist.

Although, Pastor Davis is highly favored and wonderfully blessed of the Lord, her greatest role is as a servant to His people. She desires to see the oppressed set free, heavy burdens lifted and the chains of bondage loosened so that His people can walk in their God-given purpose and destiny!!!

# *FOREWORD*

God has inspired me to write this book, part devotional and part self help manual in an attempt to minister to other believers (especially women) who are endeavoring for a true mountaintop experience on this journey called **LIFE**. God has allowed me to experience many things since I've enrolled in the school of life, some bitter and some sweet, but all surmountable by the grace and mercy of the Lord Jesus Christ. Most of these experiences were a necessary part of my personal destiny or **HER**story that eventually led to my personal growth, spiritual birth, commitment, renewal, and deliverance from a life of frustration, fruitlessness and fear.

During the past several years, as I have ministered before countless audiences, preaching and teaching the engrafted Word of God, women have come up to me after the benediction and shared their own personal **HER**story. They've testified that they were enlightened, encouraged, and often empowered to stay in the race by something that God led me to say or proclaim.

Many seemed disappointed that I didn't have a book or additional resources for them to take home to remind them of the principles that I had just shared. This realization of the needs of God's people is what gave me the impetus and inspiration to write this book.

During my own journey through life and personal **HER**story, I finally learned that if you want to soar with the eagles, you couldn't hang with buzzards all day. I also learned that you cannot stop the scavengers of life from flying over your head but you can certainly stop them from building a nest in your hair. You DO have control over your destiny if you learn from history and allow the Holy Spirit to have complete control in your life. He's not satisfied being a part of your life. He wants to BE you life.

So, the time has come! Get ready for your personal tour guide, led by the Holy Spirit, to your own mountain of fulfillment and purpose. Sit back, relax and get ready to revisit ten biblical women from Genesis to Revelation, some well known, others less prominent but all with their personal **HER**story to tell. As you read the commentary on each woman, simply ask the Holy Spirit to reveal to you the message that you need to receive from **HER**story.

Invite Jesus to join you on the pages of your own life story and allow him to use His mighty hand to delete, edit or rewrite the painful chapters from your past. Let Him dictate brand new chapters in your future that he has already begun. Remember, he already knows the wonderful ending that he has planned for you. Regardless of the story lines, smeared stains, ripped pages or red marks that you've already experienced, it's not over until God says it is over. It may be the end of a chapter (divorce, incest, unemployment, failure, etc.) but it doesn't have to be the end of the book! God has the last say-so.

I pray that this up-close-and-personal glimpse of these ten women, will encourage and empower you as you reflect on the heroines who were victors refusing to 'pause' but continuing to press toward the mark for the high calling of God in Christ Jesus.

Others, like Lot's wife, were victims who allowed Satan to pull their plug. Without the life-sustaining power of being connected to the true vine, Jesus Christ, they withered on the vine and never achieved their personal best.

All of these women, reflect some quality or vice that determined their ultimate destiny. Some allowed the enemy to pull the plug on their God-given assignment and destiny through disobedience, impatience, or some other trap that the enemy custom-made to kill, steal and destroy them. Pay close attention to their story because if you don't learn from **HER**story you're destined to repeat it!

I have rewound the tape of time and allowed you a rare opportunity to learn many valuable lessons from these historic women. After you push 'play' and begin to read about each woman, remember to press 'pause' as you read and ask the Holy Spirit to reveal to you the message that you personally need to hear from **HER**story.

# *INTRODUCTION*

The nineteenth chapter of Genesis outlines the exodus of Lot and his family from the lasciviousness and vileness of Sodom and Gomorrah to the mountain. This mountain is symbolic of the higher heights that we as believers strive for in our quest to achieve our personal destiny. This chapter chronicles the life of one families' story of excess, riotous living, lewd and perverted sexual lifestyles and disobedience to God's divine will.

The fate of Lot's wife and her ultimate bad choice of looking back made her an easy target for Satan and caused her destiny to be put on pause as she was turned into a pillar of salt. Satan pulled the plug on this woman and made her a legend and byword to this very day (as documented in Luke 17:23-24.) Luke tells us to 'remember Lot's wife' and is a gentle reminder to revisit her fatal demise in order to learn from it. If we don't learn from **HER**story, we are destined to repeat it. This particular story of Mrs. Lot's disobedience to God's command has long intrigued me from an ecclesiastical point of view and also from a woman's perspective.

The biblical account in the nineteenth chapter of Genesis gives only a fleeting glance at her home life while omitting the intimate, day-by-day details of her (obviously dysfunctional) life. What was so important to her? So enticing? So interesting? So painful? So consuming… that Mrs. Lot looked back and in the twinkling of an eye became a lifeless pillar of salt? What is **HER**story? Is **HER**story your story?

**And the men said unto Lot, Hast thou here any besides? son in law, and thy sons, and thy daughters, and whatsoever thou hast in the city, bring them out of this place: For we will destroy this place, because the cry of them is waxen great before the face of the LORD; and the LORD hath sent us to destroy it. And Lot went out, and spake unto his sons in law, which married his daughters, and said, Up, get you out of this place; for the LORD will destroy this city. But he seemed as one that mocked unto his sons in law. And when the morning arose, then the angels hastened Lot, saying, Arise, take thy wife, and thy two daughters, which are here; lest thou be consumed in the iniquity of the city. And while he lingered, the men laid hold upon his hand, and upon the hand of his wife, and upon the hand of his two daughters; the LORD being merciful unto him: and they brought him forth, and set him without the city. And it came to pass, when they had brought them forth abroad, that he said, Escape for thy life; look not behind thee, neither stay thou in all the plain; escape to the mountain, lest thou be consumed. And Lot said unto them, Oh, not so, my LORD:**

**Behold now, thy servant hath found grace in thy sight, and thou hast magnified thy mercy, which thou hast shewed unto me in saving my life; and I cannot escape to the mountain, lest some evil take me, and I die: Behold now, this city is near to flee unto, and it is a little one: Oh, let me escape thither, (is it not a little one?) and my soul shall live.**

**And he said unto him, See, I have accepted thee concerning this thing also, that I will not overthrow this city, for the which thou hast spoken. Haste thee, escape thither; for I cannot do anything till thou be come thither. Therefore the name of the city was called Zoar. The sun was risen upon the earth when Lot entered into Zoar. Then the LORD rained upon Sodom and upon Gomorrah brimstone and fire from the LORD out of heaven; And he overthrew those cities, and all the plain, and all the inhabitants of the cities, and that which grew upon the ground. But his wife looked back from behind him, and she became a pillar of salt.**

Genesis 19:12-26

**Remember Lot's wife. Whosoever shall seek to save his life shall lose it; and whosoever shall lose his life shall preserve it.**

Luke 17:23-24

What is it that keeps you from moving to your mountain? What is it that makes you feel like you're taking three steps forward and five steps backwards in your quest for fulfillment, success and purpose? According to St. John 10:10, God sent Jesus into the world so that you could have life and have it more abundantly. This abundant life will unfold daily and increasingly as you allow the Holy Spirit or Comforter to begin or continue His work within you.

**The thief cometh not, but for to steal, and to kill, and to destroy: I am come that they might have life, and that they might have it more abundantly.**

St. John 10:10

The Father has made provision through the Holy Ghost to lead and guide you as you transition from your comfort zone into the divine destiny that he has prepared for you. In other words, God wants to take you off 'pause' and 'fast forward' you into your divine destiny because 'no good thing will he withhold from them that walk uprightly.'

**For the LORD God is a sun and shield: the LORD will give grace and glory: no good thing will he withhold from them that walk uprightly.**

Psalms: 84:11

You may deny any similarity of your life **HER**story to Lot's wife and pride yourself as a woman actively involved in Sunday school, morning worship, choir practice, fifth Sunday Union meetings, women's conferences, revivals, prayer chains, and a plethora of other church related activities. You may testify that you've already attained and have already apprehended, but secretly you long for a deeper reality of the only true and living God. You have finally realized that your testimony is in the attic but your spiritual life is in the basement or somewhere in between. You occasionally toss aside the cares of this world long enough to experience the presence of God during your private prayer time or during corporate worship on Sunday mornings and Wednesday nights. These are the times that you feel free, powerful and able to run through a troop and leap over walls.

**For by thee I have run through a troop; and by my God have I leaped over a wall.**

Psalms 18:29

However, when the benediction has been given and you're no longer sheltered by the stained glass windows, the padded pews, or the fervor of the praise and worship service, the demands of everyday life and the realities of this present world often begin to flood your heart and mind---once again taking your spiritual progress hostage. What is YOUR story? Why are you still dealing with the same issues, allowing the same people to annoy you, and falling for the same tricks over and over again?

Like Lot's wife, you cannot effectively move forward as long as you're haunted by your past and are unsure of God's purpose for your future.

**And we know that all things work together for good to them that love God, to them who are the called according to his purpose.**

Romans 8:28

God wants you to 'escape to the mountain' and Satan wants to kill your joy, steal your peace and destroy the rich destiny that awaits you. He wants you to be turned into salt—so that you are profitable for nothing but to be cast out and trodden under foot.

**Ye are the salt of the earth: but if the salt have lost his savour, wherewith shall it be salted? it is thenceforth good for nothing, but to be cast out, and to be trodden under foot of men.**

Matthew 5:13

Are there times when your daily walk becomes a juggling act as you attend to the demands of life, participate in your chosen vocation and try to spend quality time with your family and God? If the answer is "yes", you are certainly not alone and are probably very aware that each of these arenas has it's own special set of pressures, expectations and needs. I can relate to Lot's wife, because I too have felt like a plate juggler riding on a roller coaster trying to survive by putting out the biggest fire first. I felt like the butcher, the baker and the candlestick maker all rolled into one while trying to be a jack-of-all-trades.

It finally dawned on me that I was not mastering anything or accomplishing very much in spite of my marathon efforts. I would often begin projects but was never able to complete them because I was operating in flesh and did not know how to plug into the power and energy of the Holy Spirit. My friends and loved ones grew increasingly dissatisfied, angry, and distant due to the small amount of time that I was able to ration out to them from my whirlwind schedule. My frustration and disappointment in myself also grew as I realized that I was just spinning my wheels and going nowhere fast.

At one phase in my life, I seemed to meet myself on the road of life while heading back to the starting line. I had to start from scratch and do a make-up test based on the same exams, quizzes and finals of life that I should have passed years ago. I tried to pass the tests of life by physical strength, emotional stability and cognitive abilities not realizing all along that it was an open book test. The Holy Bible had all of the answers from Genesis to Revelation. I had ignored the valuable lessons from history that could have helped me avoid many failures, disappointments, and heartaches. Consequently, I was continuously tripped up by the same snares and temptations wrapped in different packages but shrewdly delivered by a new UPS worker (Someone or something designed or assigned to **U**pset the **P**rogress of the **S**aint).

Often times, like the Psalmist, I have longed for wings like a dove so that I could fly away and be at rest. David continues on with, "Lo, then would I wander far off, and remain in the wilderness". Satan preys on your periods of frustrations and failures because he wants you to remain, like Lot's wife, in the wilderness—vulnerable, helpless, and hardened while the pigeons of life use you as a perch. He knows that if he keeps you at ground zero (wallowing around in self-pity) escaping your destiny instead of reshaping it, you will never soar with the eagles (Isaiah 40:31).

**And I said, Oh that I had wings like a dove! for then would I fly away, and be at rest. Lo, then would I wander far off, and remain in the wilderness. Selah. I would hasten my escape from the windy storm and tempest.**

Psalms 55:6-8

He's trying to hinder your ability to reboot and wants you to remain in the wilderness of complacency, mediocrity, fruitlessness, without zeal, passion, or direction. He does not want you to inherit your wonderful, purposeful destiny that was pre-ordained and ordered by the Lord himself.

**The steps of a good man are ordered by the LORD: and he delighteth in his way.**

Psalms 37:23

**I am the true vine, and my Father is the husbandman. Every branch in me that beareth not fruit he taketh away: and every branch that**

***beareth fruit, he purgeth it, that it may bring forth more fruit.***

St. John 15:1

For your convenience, I have used the following format in my discussion of each biblical character:

• **CHARACTER TRAIT:** For each woman depicted in this book, I have identified a specific character trait that either caused or prevented the enemy from pulling her plug and sabotaging her destiny. A brief definition of the character trait is also included from www.dictionary.com. A corresponding **HER**story Journal Page is included after each chapter.

• **BACKGROUND SCRIPTURE:** I've included the actual scriptural text (shown in italics) for your convenient reference.

• **HISTORY:** There is a brief history introducing each woman and summarizing her significance in bible history in a concise, easy to understand format.

• **HER**story: I have also included a powerful commentary related to each woman that will be helpful in your private devotions, bible study groups or women's mentoring groups.

Intertwined throughout each chapter are snippets and glimpses from the personal pages from my own life story.

Names with an * have been changed to protect the privacy of the individual or entity.

- **MEDITATION SCRIPTURES:** I've included a list of inspiring meditation scriptures on each character trait at the end of the book for your future reference, prayerful study and meditation. You are encouraged to commit these verses to memory and refer to them often.

# CHAPTER ONE

# ABIGAIL

**CHARACTER TRAIT: PERSEVERANCE** (steady persistence in a course of action, a purpose, a state, etc., esp. in spite of difficulties, obstacles, or discouragement.)

**BACKGROUND SCRIPTURE:**

*Then Abigail made haste, and took two hundred loaves, and two bottles of wine, and five sheep ready dressed, and five measures of parched corn, and an hundred clusters of raisins, and two hundred cakes of figs, and laid them on asses. And she said unto her servants, Go on before me; behold, I come after you. But she told not her husband Nabal. And it was so, as she rode on the ass, that she came down by the covert on the hill, and, behold, David and his men came down against her; and she met them. Now David had said, Surely in vain have I kept all that this fellow hath in the wilderness, so that nothing was missed of all that pertained unto him: and he hath requited me evil for good. So and more also do God unto the enemies of David, if I leave of all that pertain to him by the morning light any that pisseth against the wall. And when Abigail saw*

# HER STORY

**IF YOU DON'T LEARN FROM HERSTORY, YOU'RE DESTINED TO REPEAT IT!**

David, she hasted, and lighted off the ass, and fell before David on her face, and bowed herself to the ground, And fell at his feet, and said, Upon me, my lord, upon me let this iniquity be: and let thine handmaid, I pray thee, speak in thine audience, and hear the words of thine handmaid. Let not my lord, I pray thee, regard this man of Belial, even Nabal: for as his name is, so is he; Nabal is his name, and folly is with him: but I thine handmaid saw not the young men of my lord, whom thou didst send. Now therefore, my lord, as the LORD liveth, and as thy soul liveth, seeing the LORD hath withholden thee from coming to shed blood, and from avenging thyself with thine own hand, now let thine enemies, and they that seek evil to my lord, be as Nabal. And now this blessing which thine handmaid hath brought unto my lord, let it even be given unto the young men that follow my lord. I pray thee, forgive the trespass of thine handmaid: for the LORD will certainly make my lord a sure house; because my lord fighteth the battles of the LORD, and evil hath not been found in thee all thy days. Yet a man is risen to pursue thee, and to seek thy soul: but the soul of my lord shall be bound in the bundle of life with the LORD thy God; and the souls of thine enemies, them shall he sling out, as out of the middle of a sling. And it shall come to pass, when the LORD shall have done to my lord according to all the good that he hath spoken concerning thee, and shall have appointed thee ruler over Israel; That this shall be

**ABIGAIL**

*no grief unto thee, nor offence of heart unto my lord, either that thou hast shed blood causeless, or that my lord hath avenged himself: but when the LORD shall have dealt well with my lord, then remember thine handmaid. And David said to Abigail, Blessed be the LORD God of Israel, which sent thee this day to meet me: And blessed be thy advice, and blessed be thou, which hast kept me this day from coming to shed blood, and from avenging myself with mine own hand. For in very deed, as the LORD God of Israel liveth, which hath kept me back from hurting thee, except thou hadst hasted and come to meet me, surely there had not been left unto Nabal by the morning light any that pisseth against the wall. So David received of her hand that which she had brought him, and said unto her, Go up in peace to thine house; see, I have hearkened to thy voice, and have accepted thy person.*

1 Samuel 25:18-35

**HISTORY:** Abigail was the wife of Nabal from Carmel. When Abigail overheard Nabal's refusal to give David and his soldiers supplies to compensate them for protecting Nabal's shepherds and possessions from harm, she secretly prepared an offering and brought it to David, thanked him for his care of their property, and apologized for her husband's rudeness. This determined act of neighborly compassion touched David's heart and prompted him to change his mind about retaliating against Nabal and his entire

# HERSTORY  IF YOU DON'T LEARN FROM HERSTORY, YOU'RE DESTINED TO REPEAT IT!

household. Later, Abigail graciously accepted King David's marriage proposal after guilt-ridden Nabal suffered a sudden death at God's hand. This single, determined act catapulted her from a life of marital discord and dissatisfaction into a role of royalty and prominence.

## **HERSTORY RUN AND DON'T LOOK BACK:**

Many times you may have underestimated your own God-given power, strength and most importantly, your influence, intuition and insight. Every since the biblical documentation and often exploitation of the woman's role in the fall in the Garden of Eden, women have been portrayed as the weaker vessel in terms of physical strength and moral gullibility.

***Now the serpent was more subtil than any beast of the field which the LORD God had made. And he said unto the woman, Yea, hath God said, Ye shall not eat of every tree of the garden? And the woman said unto the serpent, We may eat of the fruit of the trees of the garden: But of the fruit of the tree which is in the midst of the garden, God hath said, Ye shall not eat of it, neither shall ye touch it, lest ye die. And the serpent said unto the woman, Ye shall not surely die: For God doth know that in the day ye eat thereof, then your eyes shall be opened, and ye shall be as gods, knowing good and evil. And when the woman saw that the tree was good for food, and that it was pleasant to the eyes, and a tree to be desired to make one wise,***

**ABIGAIL**

*she took of the fruit thereof, and did eat, and gave also unto her husband with her; and he did eat.*

Genesis 3:1-6

*Likewise, ye husbands, dwell with them according to knowledge, giving honour unto the wife, as unto the weaker vessel, and as being heirs together of the grace of life; that your prayers be not hindered.*

1 Peter 5:7

However, you are encouraged to use Abigail's triumphant rescue of her household, through an intercessory act of diplomacy, as an example of the effects and rewards of determination and action accompanied by God's supernatural intervention and favor. Never underestimate the power of the Holy Spirit that you have dwelling on the inside of you!

Greater is He that is in you than he that's in the world. As you acknowledge Jesus and rest in Him, He will direct your path and orchestrate your victory.

Thankfully, Abigail was insightful enough to see that the awful events that were about to unfold could be avoided or reversed. Although there were many obstacles in her way, Abigail devised a brilliant strategy and was able to overcome them and win the victory. Let's look at seven obstacles that she had to overcome and that you too must overcome in

**HER**STORY  IF YOU DON'T LEARN FROM **HER**STORY, YOU'RE DESTINED TO REPEAT IT!

order survive and thrive during life's cyclic phases, unpredictable stages and traumatic seasons.

**1.) NOT HAVING THE RIGHT MINDSET.** Before Abigail mounted her waiting horse, she purposed in her heart that she had to do something to save herself and her family. She was attentive to that small still voice that will also lead and guide you each time you acknowledge Him during a desperate or seemingly hopeless situation. It's imperative that you maintain a vibrant, daily and consistent relationship with the Lord through the prayer, bible study, and meditation on his word according to Psalm 1:2. A close, intimate relationship with the Lord and a keen sensitivity to the Holy Spirit will enable you (in times of distress) to enter into his presence and tap into the same caliber of power that raised Jesus Christ from the grave. As you yield to the unction and leading of the Holy Ghost, He will direct your actions and go before you to make the crooked ways straight.

**But his delight is in the law of the LORD; and in his law doth he meditate day and night.**

Psalms 1:2

**Every valley shall be filled, and every mountain and hill shall be brought low; and the crooked shall be made straight, and the rough ways shall be made smooth;**

Luke 3:5

**ABIGAIL**

**2.) TRYING TO OPERATE IN HER FLESH.** Abigail didn't depend upon her own intelligence, logic, seductiveness or wild schemes to appeal to King David. She depended on God's never-ending grace and her sincere faith that David would do the right thing. In times of trauma, disappointment, distress, or inherent failure, you too must acknowledge the Lord so that he can give you divine direction that will yield peace and victory. The battle is the Lord's as we wrestle against spiritual wickedness in high places.

**For we wrestle not against flesh and blood, but against principalities, against powers, against the rulers of the darkness of this world, against spiritual wickedness in high places.**

Ephesians 6:12

**Trust in the LORD with all thine heart; and lean not unto thine own understanding. In all thy ways acknowledge him, and he shall direct thy paths.**

Proverbs 3:5-6

**3.) GOING EMPTY-HANDED:** Regardless of how inferior, uneducated, disabled, shy, self-conscious, or inferior that you may think you are, there is always something within you that you can give to bring about a victory in any situation. As you seek the face of the Lord, he will direct you to make a phone call, contact an associate, go on a fast, or ask for forgiveness. Most of the time, the Lord will lead you to sow a seed that you already possess to multiply your peace, faith

# HERSTORY

*IF YOU DON'T LEARN FROM HERSTORY, YOU'RE DESTINED TO REPEAT IT!*

or favor and ultimately solve a problem that you've faced.

**Then Abigail made haste, and took two hundred loaves, and two bottles of wine, and five sheep ready dressed, and five measures of parched corn, and an hundred clusters of raisins, and two hundred cakes of figs, and laid them on asses.**

1 Samuel 25:18

**4.) ALLOWING OTHERS TO DISTRACT HER.** She did not allow others to shake her faith and cause her to doubt that she was doing the right thing. You too may have to be a Lone Ranger during times of spiritual warfare. Sometimes it's best not to tell anyone of your plans once God has directed you to do something that might be considered radical or different from the status quo. When your behavior is no longer predictable, people will be uncomfortable and will often try to dissuade or hinder you.

People are intimidated by **NEXT LEVEL** people and are usually comfortable with **SAME LEVEL** people. "Who does she think she is"? "What is she trying to prove?" are all questions that people will ask when you get out of your comfort zone and begin to step out in faith. Let Abigail be a model for you as you saddle your horse of faith and ride like the wind into unknown territory, bridled by the reins of courage and harnessed with a meek, quiet spirit.

**ABIGAIL**

## 5.) BEING DECEIVED INTO CHANGING DIRECTIONS DURING THE TRIP.
I recently read a true story about a lady who lived alone and perished in a horrific house fire. The brave firefighters found her about two feet from the back door. If she had pressed on a little longer, maybe she would have survived. So many times, victory is just around the corner but we allow the enemy to bring fear into our hearts, faint in our spirit and trick us into taking our hands off of the gospel plow. The sixth chapter of Ephesians reminds us to stand firm and refuse to change courses. Once God leads you into a plan of deliverance, stand on his word. Like Abigail, you must run and refuse to look back!!!

This is the same lesson that I had to teach my own daughter, Krystal, when she put the honeymoon before the wedding and became pregnant out of wedlock. She became pregnant as a freshman at Tallahassee Community College. After my grandson Kayden, was born, she had an extremely difficult time juggling school, work, study, finals, household chores, late night feedings, and the myriad of tasks involved in balancing child-rearing and college courses.

She would often complain to me that it was "too hard" and "I don't think I can make it." I gave her as much moral and financial support as I could in spite of my absorption with the care of my elderly mother and learning-disabled daughter, that consumed much of my time. I finally drew a proverbial line in the sand one Sunday evening after refusing her invitation to

# HERSTORY
**IF YOU DON'T LEARN FROM HERSTORY, YOU'RE DESTINED TO REPEAT IT!**

yet another pity party to bemoan her over-worked existence. "Okay, Krystal" I said. "Why don't you just drop out then? I know for a fact that they need someone to flip hamburgers at the local *McBerries. Maybe college is too hard for you right now. You can go to college after the baby has grown up and things are not quite so difficult for you." Her eyes grew wide and her expression changed from defeat and despair to one of tenacity and determination as she declared, "I can do it Mom. I know I can. I don't want to drop out." I said, " Okay! Go for it!"

Currently, she holds a Bachelor's degree in English and Spanish from Florida State University and has taught middle school English for two years. She leads the praise and worship services at New Destiny Church and is currently working on producing an original CD of inspirational songs of praise and worship. Her son completed Kindergarten this year and is active in the ministry at our church, New Destiny. If Satan had succeeded into tricking her into changing directions in the middle of the trip, she might still be at the nationally known eatery helping customers in the drive-thorough line saying, "Hello, how about a Value Meal with a large Coke and a hot apple pie?"

**Wherefore take unto you the whole armour of God, that ye may be able to withstand in the evil day, and having done all, to stand. Stand therefore, having your loins girt about with truth, and having on the breastplate of righteousness;**

Ephesians 6:13,14

*ABIGAIL*

## 6.) NOT CONTINUING AT A STEADY PACE AND BEING FULLY COMMITTED:
1 Corinthians 15:58 reminds us to," be ye stedfast, unmoveable, always abounding in the work of the Lord, forasmuch as ye know that your labour is not in vain in the Lord." There may be times that you feel that you are not making any progress at all. It may seem that you are taking three steps forward and five backwards. No doubt, Abigail felt that she wouldn't get to King David in time. Nevertheless, she continued at a steady pace until she was face to face with the king. Persistence and perseverance are essential even in the face of fatigue, discouragement or doubt. Even if the outlook seems bleak, you must continue to press forward with your eyes fastened on Jesus.

*Therefore, my beloved brethren, be ye stedfast, unmoveable, always abounding in the work of the Lord, forasmuch as ye know that your labour is not in vain in the Lord.*

1 Corinthians 15:58

MY PERSONAL **HER**STORY PAGE

## *PERSEVERANCE*

> *"Are there times when your daily walk becomes a juggling act as you attend to the demands of life, participate in your chosen vocation and try to spend quality time with your family and God?"*

**Please list below the things that are creating the greatest demands on your time and energy:**

_____

_____

_____

_____

_____

_____

_____

_____

_____

CHAPTER TWO

# *ANNA*

**CHARACTER TRAIT: ASSURANCE/FOCUS** (To adjust one's vision or an optical device so as to render a clear, distinct image; To concentrate attention or energy.)

**BACKGROUND SCRIPTURE:**

*And there was one Anna, a prophetess, the daughter of Phanuel, of the tribe of Aser: she was of a great age, and had lived with an husband seven years from her virginity; And she was a widow of about fourscore and four years, which departed not from the temple, but served God with fastings and prayers night and day. And she coming in that instant gave thanks likewise unto the Lord, and spake of him to all them that looked for redemption in Jerusalem.*

St. Luke 2:36-38

**HISTORY:** For seven years, Anna was married before becoming a widow. She remained single even though the scripture tells us that she married in her "maidenhood". She was eighty-four years old and remained in the Temple serving God by day and by

# HER**STORY**

**IF YOU DON'T LEARN FROM HER**STORY, YOU'RE DESTINED TO REPEAT IT!

night through fasting and prayer. She was elated when she finally got a chance to see the forty-day old baby Jesus during the time that Mary and Joseph brought him into the Temple (it was the custom to bring the firstborn) to be redeemed.

She used this opportunity to tell all of the people who were still waiting for the promised Messiah to come that God had already sent the Savior in the form of his only begotten son Jesus!

## **HERSTORY: "MINE EYES HAVE SEEN THE GLORY"**

Anna waited patiently and kept her **focus** even when those around her were adamant that (although he was cute and cuddly) the infant Jesus was not the promised Messiah. As they continued to deny the deity of Christ and look for the long prophesied Messiah, Anna remained satisfied and convinced that she had indeed seen Him in the dimpled face of the Prince of Peace, King of Kings and Lord of Lords. Let's look at the importance of maintaining focus and assurance when everything and everyone around you is preaching, teaching, practicing and supporting a different doctrine, mindset and belief system.

There will be seasons when you will be have to stand alone when even your own family, closest friends or church associates can't or refuse to see the vision or assignment that God has so vividly shown you. Many times their eyes are simply blinded by the spirit of jealousy and inferiority. This is why it is so important to have an intimate relationship with Christ so that you can hear his voice and have the confidence of Anna to speak up and work out your own soul salvation with fear and trembling. There will be seasons when you will find yourself a Lone Ranger as you stand in spite of, in defiance of, in allegiance to or because of a God-given conviction or stance. It is crucial to make sure that you are right and having done all to stand—**STAND THEREFORE.**

Like Anna, I had a personal experience with the Lord during a visit to Rochester, New York in the late seventies and have been standing with assurance ever since. At the time, I was a young, Florida State University co-ed (still wet behind the ears) living in Tallahassee, Florida---the farthest that I had ever traveled away from my hometown of Greenwood, Florida (a small, rural community about nine miles from Marianna, Florida). I was so excited about expanding my territory and going north while finally getting an opportunity to fly on a real airplane. I was ecstatic about spending time with my sister Mattie, her husband Jerome, their 4 year-old son, Jerome, Jr. and the opportunity to spend the whole summer in New, York.

I really thought I was hot stuff as I packed my new hot pants, halters and chic mini skirts. I was ready for the nightlife with a New York flavor. Finally, I would see what my brother-in-law had been talking about when he visited us in Florida. Little did I know that my brother-in-law had just recently received the baptism of the Holy Spirit a couple of weeks before I arrived and was on fire for the Lord.

Immediately, he began to witness to me and invited me to attend Thursday night prayer service at his church.

Reluctantly, I agreed to attend and found myself totally caught up in the anointing and power of the Holy Spirit from the moment that I walked into Bibleway Healing Temple. The pastor, Dr. Eula Mae Nelson, was preaching under a heavy anointing as the glory of God filled the house. Well, the rest is history! The Lord saved me that same night, and filled me with the Holy Ghost with evidence of speaking in tongues. I was filled with a supernatural love and peace that surpasses all understanding. I was baptized in water the same night, rose up to walk in the newness of life and have never been the same since. I have a calm assurance that I too have seen the Messiah.

**Wherefore, my beloved, as ye have always obeyed, not as in my presence only, but now much more in my absence, work out your own salvation with fear and trembling.**

Philippians: 2:12

There have been numerous times that the Lord instructed me to do something and at the time it seemed nearly impossible or unattainable. One thing that I've learned over the years is that if Satan can't make you slow down, he'll try to make you go too fast causing you to operate out of season. Timing is very important in seeing the fruit of your labor, the manifestation of your dreams and the success of your projects.

There are many things that the enemy will use to abort your dreams and pull the plug on you if you are not focused and steadfast in your endeavors. Like Anna, you must learn to 'see' Jesus when everything and everyone around you points to something else—something more logical, easily attained or politically correct.

**But God hath chosen the foolish things of the world to confound the wise; and God hath chosen the weak things of the world to confound those which are mighty; 1 Corinthians 1:27**

Like Anna, you need to constantly maintain your focus so that you can see Jesus in His fullness, majesty and glory. Let's look at two critical elements that are crucial to maintaining your focus so that you can resist the enemy causing him to flee from you.

### • YOU MUST SEE IT BY FAITH:

**Paul reminds us that ...faith is the substance of things hoped for, the evidence of things not seen.**

Hebrews 11:1

This principle reminds me of the time over 20 years ago, when my youngest daughter, Kadriane, was 2 ½ years old and began to frequently bump into

# HER STORY

**IF YOU DON'T LEARN FROM HERSTORY, YOU'RE DESTINED TO REPEAT IT!**

furniture and trip over toys around our home. She was a beautiful, normal baby when she was born and had been given a clean bill of health by her pediatrician, *Dr. Sarah Manning. I grew quite concerned and could not imagine what was happening to my playful, fun-loving toddler. Immediately, I made an appointment for Kadriane at a local eye clinic to see if she needed glasses. I had no clue that the events that were about to unfold would radically change our lives forever.

As scheduled, Kadriane and I arrived at the ophthalmologist's office where *Dr. John Lowe carefully and lovingly examined her. Unfortunately, after all of his tests and probing, he was unable to come up with a definitive diagnosis regarding her apparent visual difficulties. He referred her for a CAT scan at the nearby hospital to see if there was something that he had missed during his extensive examination.

A few days later, Kadriane and I showed up for a consultation with *Dr. Jacob Huckleberry, a prominent neurologist, who has since retired. I shared my concerns as he reviewed the referral from *Dr. John Lowe, the ophthalmologist. He quickly filled out the necessary paperwork and sent us over to the Radiology department of the hospital for a CAT scan.

After Kadriane was sedated and dye infused into her tiny veins, the CAT scan began. I was allowed to stay in the room, but had to wear a lead apron to protect myself from the harmful effects of the radiation. From my seat, I could see the technician as he clicked dials, punched buttons and pushed and twisted knobs for what seemed like an eternity. Suddenly, his eyes grew huge and he began beckoning frantically for his fellow technicians to "come and look". Soon there was a rather ominous group of medical staff gathered around the monitor. When the scan finally ended, the technician nervously asked me to go directly back to *Dr. Huckleberry's office and to remain in the building and wait until his office reopened after lunch. Since the office was closed for lunch, it looked like a ghost town by the time that Kadriane and I arrived. As instructed, I just sat there in the quietness of my surroundings and waited for the office staff and *Dr. Huckleberry to return and discuss the CAT scan results.

Kadriane was sound asleep in my arms due to the sedation that was administered to calm her during the scan. What turned out to be an hour-long wait seemed like an eternity as a million thoughts raced through my mind. Why did the technician ask me not to leave the hospital? Why was he so nervous as he spoke to me? Why did he call so many of his colleagues to look at the monitor while he was doing the scan? What had they seen? What had caused my child's vision to fail so quickly and suddenly? Soon the nurse came to the door of the waiting room and called, "Kadriane Davis" and jolted me from my sea of uncertainty, fear and doubt. Dr. Huckleberry looked me straight in the eye and said, "Ms. Davis, Kadriane has a craniophyringioma and we've GOT to do surgery!" I said, "Oh, maybe I can schedule it for sometimes

# **HER**STORY

**IF YOU DON'T LEARN FROM *HER*STORY, YOU'RE DESTINED TO REPEAT IT!**

during the summer because I'm a teacher and will be on summer break soon."

He said, "You don't understand, you need to go home and get some clothes and come back and check her into the hospital this evening. Your child has a brain tumor the size of a lemon and she could be dead in a week if we don't move fast." Before I left the doctor's office, I called my school and told my principal about the current state of affairs. I went home and shared the news with my mother and Krystal. I telephoned and shared the news with my extended family around the country, bible study members and church family. I called her father in Marianna while I was still in a state of shock and broke the news to him. He too expressed disbelief and sadness and said that he would be unable to come to visit her but would "pray for us". Thank God that there is no distance in prayer.

To make a long story short, we arrived at the hospital, checked in and Kadriane was whisked off for a whirlwind pace of tests and pre-surgery assessments. The neurologist showed me her x-ray and I almost passed out when I saw the tumor almost the size of a lemon that had taken my daughter's brain hostage. He stressed the wisdom and urgency in not delaying surgery because the tumor seemed to be growing viciously and he feared for her life. I immediately began to pray and God allowed me to see Jesus instead of the tumor. He began to remind me of Jesus' promises in His word and each time that one of the specialists would come in and give a prophecy of doom and despair, I would replace it with a scriptural promise of hope and peace. If Satan can define you, he will confine you! Don't let Satan box you in.

Kadriane and I finally ended up in Memphis, Tennessee where my sister Mittie, her husband Abe, and their two sons, Derek and Abe III had recently moved. We ended up in Memphis because the neurologist and surgeons in Tallahassee were predicting that she might not survive the surgery and if she did, she would be totally blind and possibly a "vegetable". Their prognosis only gave her a five to ten percent chance of survival.

I thank God to this day for placing my sister Mittie in Memphis for 'such a time as this'. Mittie had watched a dramatic, television documentary about a young girl from India who had been bitten by a rare, but deadly snake. This painful snakebite almost caused her to lose her leg and her life. The girl underwent emergency surgery at the hospital and by the grace of God, he used the surgeon, nurses and other hospital staff to save the girl's life and leg. Halleluiah!

Mittie immediately went on a fact-finding mission, made some phone calls and gathered the contact information that I needed to get in touch with the girl's heroic surgeon, *Dr. Alex Bently. After listening to my plight, and realizing that Kadriane's life was slowly ebbing away with each passing moment, he agreed to perform the surgery.

# HERSTORY  IF YOU DON'T LEARN FROM *HER*STORY, YOU'RE DESTINED TO REPEAT IT!

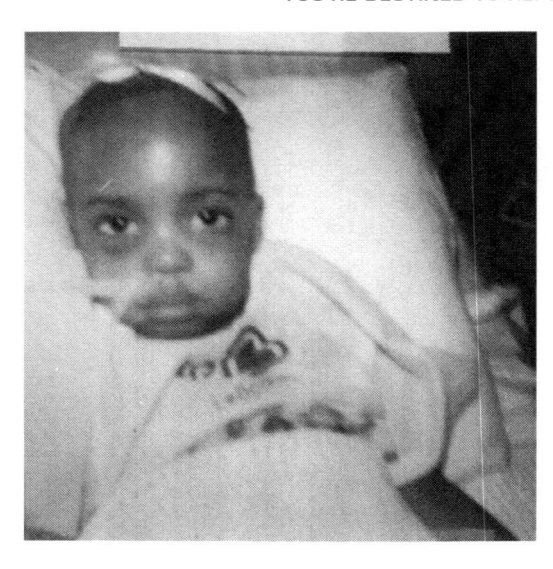

*This is Kadriane shortly after undergoing an 11 hour brain surgery in Memphis, Tennessee.*

Two days later, Kadriane and I boarded a jet on our way to Memphis, Tennessee. I almost missed our flight due to a layover in Atlanta and had to run frantically while carrying Kadriane and an over-stuffed bag on my shoulder. We finally managed to reach our seats near the rear of the plane approximately two minutes before the flight attendant announced, "Please buckle your seatbelts, we are preparing for take-off."

On March 27, 1987, Kadriane underwent an 11-hour surgery to remove the tumor that had taken up residency on her optic nerve (now we know why her vision was failing so rapidly and mysteriously) near her pituitary gland and brain stem. The Tallahassee doctor had prophesied that she could lose her sight if the optic nerve was severed. As he had predicted, she went totally blind immediately after surgery and for about two months remained blind and fearful of falling.

She had severe nystagmus (which means that her eyeballs seemed to dance in their sockets) and used her hands and fingers to cautiously explore the world around her. I refused to accept her blindness but continued to call those things that were not as if they were. I thanked God daily for her normal vision (by faith) and she gradually began to regain her sight in the right eye. Her vision is certainly not 20/20 but she is able to read, watch television, and ambulate freely in familiar areas. **"Faith IS the substance of things hoped for and the evidence of things not seen".**

She had a couple of petit mal seizures shortly after surgery but began to have horrific grand mal seizures around the age of eight. Shortly thereafter she began a complex regime of anti-seizure medications— many with devastating side effects such as violent mood swings and uncontrollable anger. She had an extremely difficult time at school due to her non-compliant behavior, compulsive-obsessive tendencies, and chronic seizure disorder. The administrators, teachers and staff at her various schools were absolutely wonderful and tried diligently to minimize the times that they had to contact me at work to report another seizure or attack on a teacher.

I too experienced physical attacks from Kadriane as she wrestled with the effects of the seizure medications needed to sustain her life. Paradoxically, the very medicines that stopped the seizures caused her to be angry and moody. I remember many times in the middle of morning worship at Tabernacle Church,

# HER STORY

**IF YOU DON'T LEARN FROM *HER*STORY, YOU'RE DESTINED TO REPEAT IT!**

(where I was a member for many years before I founded New Destiny) I had to run out of the sanctuary and catch Kadriane before she ran out into the street. She would become enraged from the denial of a request (like wanting to sing on the microphone or go out and buy some chips) or if I asked her to sit still.

On another occasion, we were leaving a doctor's appointment and Kadriane jerked away from me and fell down a 10-foot ravine that fortunately was dry due to lack of rain. I instinctively slid down to rescue her but could not get back to the top due to its depth and the cumbersomeness of trying to hold on to Kadriane. A kind-hearted stranger heard my cries for help and climbed down and pulled both of us out. When we finally got into the car, she said nothing about our near brush with death, but continued to inquire about the chicken nugget meal. The side effects from the medicines had caused her to lose reason and self-control.

In retrospect, I realize that Satan used this turbulent season in my life to cause me to lose my focus and my testimony. If the enemy cannot gain territory with you, he will attack those closest to you as a distraction. Well, because God is faithful, I held on to His unchanging hand, kept my focus (like Anna) and Kadriane is alive today. She is well behaved in social settings, lives each day to the fullest, sings solos in church, has impeccable speech, and loves computers, word searches and reading. She celebrates life to the fullest, loves her family and friends as God continues to restore what the enemy tried to destroy.

During the darkest chapter in **HER**story, she would have six to seven seizures a day that were so severe that the teachers had to call 911 at school. She spent an average of 3-4 weeks every year in the hospital and was a frequent visitor in the school clinic. Today, she is almost seizure free because of the blood of Jesus and his marvelous grace.

### • YOU MUST TASTE AND SEE FOR YOURSELF:

The Psalmist shares an important truth when he encourages the reader to taste and see that the Lord is good.

***O taste and see that the LORD is good: blessed is the man that trusteth in him.***

Psalms 34:8

Regardless of how many women's conferences you have attended, how many morning devotionals you have purchased or how many sermonettes and books you've ordered from Christian television, nothing can take the place of personal experience. You've got to taste the sweet grace and mercy of Jesus for yourself. Remember, **MERCY** is not getting punished for the things that you know in your heart you deserve to be punished for and **GRACE** is receiving the gifts and favor from the Lord that you know that you don't deserve.

# HERSTORY
**IF YOU DON'T LEARN FROM HERSTORY, YOU'RE DESTINED TO REPEAT IT!**

When the Lord pays your bond and bails you out of a situation where you were between a rock and a hard place with no way out, it becomes an appetizer of his goodness and sweetness. Then, the next time that you're in trouble or in travail, you'll remember the sweet taste of his grace and mercy. One mistake that Satan makes is letting the children of God get some experience under their belt. Now that I have tasted and seen the goodness of God time and time again, nobody can tell me anything. I am fully persuaded that nothing can separate me from the love of God, which is in Christ Jesus.

**Nay, in all these things we are more than conquerors through him that loved us. For I am persuaded, that neither death, nor life, nor angels, nor principalities, nor powers, nor things present, nor things to come, Nor height, nor depth, nor any other creature, shall be able to separate us from the love of God, which is in Christ Jesus our Lord.**

Romans 8:37-39

MY PERSONAL *HER*STORY PAGE

# ASSURANCE/FOCUS

> *"There are many things that the enemy will use to abort your dreams and pull the plug on you if you are not focused and steadfast in your endeavors."*

**What are your dreams? What would you do if you didn't have any issues with money? What would you do during the next chapter of your life if you knew that you couldn't fail?**

_____
_____
_____
_____
_____
_____
_____
_____
_____
_____

CHAPTER THREE

# *DEBORAH*

**CHARACTER TRAIT: COURAGE** (the quality of mind or spirit that enables a person to face difficulty, danger, pain, etc., without fear; bravery)

**BACKGROUND SCRIPTURE:**

*And she sent and called Barak the son of Abinoam out of Kedeshnaphtali, and said unto him, Hath not the LORD God of Israel commanded, saying, Go and draw toward mount Tabor, and take with thee ten thousand men of the children of Naphtali and of the children of Zebulun? And I will draw unto thee to the river Kishon Sisera, the captain of Jabin's army, with his chariots and his multitude; and I will deliver him into thine hand. And Barak said unto her, If thou wilt go with me, then I will go: but if thou wilt not go with me, then I will not go. And she said, I will surely go with thee: notwithstanding the journey that thou takest shall not be for thine honour; for the LORD shall sell Sisera into the hand of a woman. And Deborah arose, and went with Barak to Kedesh.*

Judges 4:6-9

# HERSTORY
**IF YOU DON'T LEARN FROM *HER*STORY, YOU'RE DESTINED TO REPEAT IT!**

**HISTORY:** Deborah was a judge and a prophetess who told Barak of God's command to march with ten thousand men to Mount Tabor to destroy Sisera (the leader of the Caanite oppressor, Jabin). Barak refused to go alone but demanded Deborah's presence. She agreed to do it his way, but admonished him that God would deliver Sisera into the hands of a woman who, instead of him, would get the glory.

## **HERSTORY:** WHAT'S YOUR ASSIGNMENT?

One day, I walked into my principal's office and noticed a simple but poignant poster on his wall. It simply stated, "The only thing that is constant is change itself". God used it to speak volumes to my spirit.

So many times we remain in a comfort zone of familiarity, predictability and complacency. We

*Krystal and Kadriane playing 'house' on Ridgeway Steet (Her hair had been shaved for surgery.)*

become satisfied with the status quo because there is safety in familiarity. Think about it. You probably travel the same route to your job each morning without even thinking about it. You may sit in the same pew at church that you have sat in for years and listen to the same choir songs and leave at the same spiritual level that you entered.

No doubt, Deborah was comfortable with the historical military structure of the male-dominated military coups and attacks. After all, women were considered and treated as the weaker vessel. Nevertheless, Deborah demonstrated great courage in the following arenas:

**1.) SHE DARED TO OBEY THE VOICE OF GOD:**
Deborah had a relationship with God that allowed her to recognize his voice and move forward with confidence and courage at his command. When she heard the military instructions straight from the lips of almighty God, she immediately shared the instructions that she had heard with Barak. She was not deterred when Barak hesitated and refused to step up to the plate. Neither did she back down when she realized that God's assignment must be carried out even if the plans needed to be fine-tuned or changed. She accepted Barak's challenge to join the fight.

In the late eighties, our family moved to Tallahassee, Florida, a few years before my daughter's brain surgery. Not knowing much about the real estate market in Tallahassee, I ended up purchasing a twenty-

# HER STORY

**IF YOU DON'T LEARN FROM HERSTORY, YOU'RE DESTINED TO REPEAT IT!**

five year old house on Ridgeway Street. From the beginning, I realized that I had purchased a lemon and during Tallahassee's first winter we almost froze to death due to a malfunctioning furnace and poor insulation. We stayed on Ridgeway Street for three years while I tried to patch up the house through a series of expensive repairs and upgrades. When I had one thing repaired, something else would tear up. In three short years, I had to have a new roof, new flooring, a new central heat and air system, new plumbing, spend $500 for the removal of a rotten oak tree and the list goes on. Since this was a source of contention and aggravation to me, I began to seek the Lord about my dilemma. "How could I get ahead financially if I had to continue to pour money into this old house?", I prayed.

As I prayed and meditated on God's words and promises, I began to sense an urgency in my spirit to purchase a newer home. I began to read in Deuteronomy 28 about the blessings promised to those who hearken to the voice of the Lord and soon I knew for a certainty that God had assigned me to build a house from the ground up.

**And it shall come to pass, if thou shalt hearken diligently unto the voice of the LORD thy God, to observe and to do all his commandments which I command thee this day, that the LORD thy God will set thee on high above all nations of the earth: And all these blessings shall come on thee, and overtake thee, if thou shalt hearken unto the voice**

of the LORD thy God. Blessed shalt thou be in the city, and blessed shalt thou be in the field. Blessed shall be the fruit of thy body, and the fruit of thy ground, and the fruit of thy cattle, the increase of thy kine, and the flocks of thy sheep. Blessed shall be thy basket and thy store. Blessed shalt thou be when thou comest in, and blessed shalt thou be when thou goest out. The LORD shall cause thine enemies that rise up against thee to be smitten before thy face: they shall come out against thee one way, and flee before thee seven ways. The LORD shall command the blessing upon thee in thy storehouses, and in all that thou settest thine hand unto; and he shall bless thee in the land which the LORD thy God giveth thee. The LORD shall establish thee an holy people unto himself, as he hath sworn unto thee, if thou shalt keep the commandments of the LORD thy God, and walk in his ways. And all people of the earth shall see that thou art called by the name of the LORD; and they shall be afraid of thee. And the LORD shall make thee plenteous in goods, in the fruit of thy body, and in the fruit of thy cattle, and in the fruit of thy ground, in the land which the LORD sware unto thy fathers to give thee. The LORD shall open unto thee his good treasure, the heaven to give the rain unto thy land in his season, and to bless all the work of thine hand: and thou shalt lend unto many nations, and thou shalt not borrow. And the LORD shall make thee the head, and not the tail; and thou shalt be above only, and thou

# HERSTORY
**IF YOU DON'T LEARN FROM HERSTORY, YOU'RE DESTINED TO REPEAT IT!**

***shalt not be beneath; if that thou hearken unto the commandments of the LORD thy God, which I command thee this day, to observe and to do them:***

Deuteronomy 28:1-13

Please understand that I was a divorced mother of two and had no prior knowledge of blueprints, subcontractors, surveys, or the myriad of steps involved in constructing a house. I had heard horror stories from male and female friends who had been victimized by shoddy work, dishonest contractors, and legal problems. I'd also heard of sub-contractors who prolonged the building project by not showing up for work because they were somewhere else working on bigger, more expensive projects. I was warned by well-meaning friends and loved ones that I was foolish to attempt such a male-dominated task.

In less than a year, God allowed our family to move into a brand new, 4 bedroom, home and today I only have a few more years on the mortgage before it's paid off. I listened to the voice of the Lord and now I give Jesus all the glory for the successful completion of this assignment. To God be the Glory!

## 2.) SHE VERBALLY DECREED THE VICTORY:

Deborah told Barak that a woman would get the victory. She called those things that were not as if they were. Yes! The words that we speak can help birth blessings and victories in the spiritual realm.

Even when things may seem bleak or hopeless in the natural realm, we must continue to stand on God's word. God said it and that settles it. We must speak or repeat (Like Deborah did to Barak) God's commandments and promises when we are entering into spiritual warfare. Sometimes God sends us into unknown or foreign territory and we will fail if we do not realize that God is above situations and circumstances.

Speak to your situation and decree the victory! Remember that God has authority over:

- **TIME:** *But, beloved, be not ignorant of this one thing, that one day is with the Lord as a thousand years, and a thousand years as one day.*

    2 Peter 3:8

- **NATURAL ORDER:** *Abraham fell facedown; he laughed and said to himself, "Will a son be born to a man a hundred years old? Will Sarah bear a child at the age of ninety?"*

    Genesis 17:17

- **QUALITY:** *And saith unto him, Every man at the beginning doth set forth good wine; and when men have well drunk, then that which is worse: but thou hast kept the good wine until now.*

    St. John 2:10

**HER**STORY   IF YOU DON'T LEARN FROM **HER**STORY, YOU'RE DESTINED TO REPEAT IT!

- **QUANTITY:** *And when it was evening, his disciples came to him, saying, This is a desert place, and the time is now past; send the multitude away, that they may go into the villages, and buy themselves victuals. But Jesus said unto them, They need not depart; give ye them to eat. And they say unto him, We have here but five loaves, and two fishes. He said, Bring them hither to me. And he commanded the multitude to sit down on the grass, and took the five loaves, and the two fishes, and looking up to heaven, he blessed, and brake, and gave the loaves to his disciples, and the disciples to the multitude. And they did all eat, and were filled: and they took up of the fragments that remained twelve baskets full.*

    Matthew 14:15-20

- **DISTANCE:** *The power of the LORD came upon Elijah and, tucking his cloak into his belt, he ran ahead of Ahab all the way to Jezreel.*

    I Kings 18:46

- **DEATH:** *So when this corruptible shall have put on incorruption, and this mortal shall have put on immortality, then shall be brought to pass the saying that is written, Death is swallowed up in victory*

    1 Corinthians 15:54

MY PERSONAL **HER**STORY PAGE

## COURAGE

> *"So many times we remain in a comfort zone of familiarity, predictability and complacency."*

**What are some things in your life that need to be changed?**

_____
_____
_____
_____
_____
_____
_____
_____
_____

CHAPTER FOUR

# *ESTHER*

**CHARACTER TRAIT: BOLDNESS** (not hesitating or fearful in the face of actual or possible danger or rebuff; courageous and daring: *a bold hero*.)

**BACKGROUND SCRIPTURE:** The entire book of Esther

**HISTORY:** Her uncle Mordecai, who was an official in the court of King Xerxes, raised Esther, an orphan. She was chosen for the royal harem after King Xexes banished Queen Vashiti. She was the king's favorite and was chosen to be his queen. She was later able to save the king's life after she reminded King Xerxes of her uncle Mordecai's report to her of an assassination plot, thereby saving his life. She also demonstrated boldness (when evil Haman decided to exterminate the Jews,) by making a bold plea to the king and ultimately saving her people from annihilation.

**HERSTORY: "OH!"**

There have been many times that I have been puzzled or confused about a particular situation or circumstance and have spent restless days and sleepless nights trying to figure things out on my own. Suddenly, seemingly out of the blue, a light bulb would come on in my mind and I could clearly see the solution or answer that I had been seeking. I would say to myself, **"OH"**!

This is the stage that Queen Esther came to when she realized that she was indeed the one who was chosen for 'such a time as this' to speak to her husband, King Xerxes, and save her people from being destroyed. Queen Esther was successful after she came to the end of herself and decided "if I perish, let me perish, I am going to see the king". If she had never had this 'OH' moment, the enemy could have pulled the plug on her AND her people.

Let's take a moment and look at some other "OH" moments that are important in preventing the enemy from pulling the plug on you:

• **<u>OKAY, LORD:</u>** It is necessary to totally obey and trust the Lord even if it is contrary to your own feelings, opinions, desires or thoughts. I can remember the times that the Lord has directed me to start a fast on the day of the school Christmas party and I had to obey even though I was looking forward to all of the homemade casseroles and desserts.

There have been other times when I have been on the phone with a friend, church member or co-worker and the Lord will direct me to get off the phone and read my bible or commune with him just when the conversation was most interesting. I learned early in my Christian experience that obedience is better than sacrifice.

You too must be sensitive to the leading of the Holy Spirit at all times. When He places an unction in your spirit to do something and you ignore or disobey him, it greatly grieves him. He will not force himself on you and eventually your spiritual perception will be dull or non-existent. Your spiritual plug has just been pulled!

- **OPEN UP:** Esther was able to open up to King Xerxes and tell him the truth about her own Jewish heritage and the evil plan of Haman, the man that he trusted greatly. Like Esther, you must realize that your job, possessions, church title or family heritage do not define who you are. If you let these things define you, they will eventually confine you and pull the plug on your destiny. Galatians 2:20 reminds us clearly about this life that we now live in the flesh.

*This is my grandmother, Ella Jackson, who lost her brave fight with breast cancer in 1978.*

# **HER**STORY
**IF YOU DON'T LEARN FROM *HER*STORY, YOU'RE DESTINED TO REPEAT IT!**

**I am crucified with Christ: nevertheless I live; yet not I, but Christ liveth in me: and the life which I now live in the flesh I live by the faith of the Son of God, who loved me, and gave himself for me.**

Galatians 2:20

There have been many times in my own life that I've had to get up- close-and-personal with God and just pour out my heart to him. When my grandmother, Ella Jackson, was diagnosed with breast cancer it was a sad day in our family. We learned, rather unceremoniously, that my grandmother had been secretly nursing a large lump in her breast for years until it finally doubled in size, ruptured and turned her breast into a grotesque, grayish, grapefruit-sized mass. We were sitting on our front porch one cool, August evening when a severed blood vessel in my grandmother's diseased breast caused a massive hemorrhage. The blood was so profuse that it pooled and ran off the side of the porch. At last, her carefully guarded secret was out as she sheepishly waited for the ambulance while we tried unrelentlessly to stop the bleeding, conceal our fear and comfort her at the same time.

After the ambulance rushed her to the hospital, we waited for hours for *Dr. William Donald to complete his examination and confer with our family members regarding treatment options. I watched the look of fear and helplessness on my own mother's face as he predicted that my grandmother had only a few months to live. He agreed to do a total mastectomy so that her last days would be comfortable and to eliminate the awful stench that she had lived with each time she removed her homemade bandages from her decaying breast.

I was totally devastated and asked God many questions. Why didn't we suspect something was wrong? How could we live in the same house with a woman and not know that she had such a deadly secret? What made her feel that she could not share with her loving, supportive family? What had we done to make her feel this way? How could I live without Grand? (The name that all of her grandchildren so affectionately called her). The open-ended questions continued as I stood before her open casket at Greenwood Chapel AME church one cold December morning and asked, "Why didn't God heal her?" "Why do bad things happen to good people?" and "What now?". I thought that my pain would last forever. Now, over 30 years later, I can write about my grandmother, talk and laugh over some of her humorous antics and even look at old pictures without a hint of a tear or remorse.

Even though you may be dealing with a painful situation of your own right now and it seems that you will never pass through this season in your life, you must say, "Okay Lord, it's in your hand". I know that you are not going to put any more on me than I can bear. If I perish, let me perish, I'm going through and I'm coming out more than a conqueror. If he allows

# **HER**STORY

**IF YOU DON'T LEARN FROM HERSTORY, YOU'RE DESTINED TO REPEAT IT!**

Satan to bring you to it, He will take you through it—even as you walk through the valley of the shadow of death (Psalms 23).

**There hath no temptation taken you but such as is common to man: but God is faithful, who will not suffer you to be tempted above that ye are able; but will with the temptation also make a way to escape, that ye may be able to bear it.**

1 Corinthians 10:13

- **OCCUPY:** Any trip to the rain forest will reveal it's beautiful, lush foliage including many species of fern and majestic bamboos. It is amazing that if you plant fern seeds in the rain forest, give them water, they will sprout and grow quickly and cover the earth very quickly. On the other hand, a bamboo seed takes five years to even come up. After the bamboo seed finally sprouts up, it is still smaller than a fern, but in just six short months, it will grow to a height of over 100 feet tall. The bamboo had spent the first five years growing roots.

Esther had been raised properly in the house of her uncle Mordecai before she was chosen to be queen and also spent a year of preparation and training before she was even brought before the king, ultimately winning his heart and favor. Like Esther, you too must be prepared to wait on the Lord or occupy until he comes. Isaiah 40:31 encourages us with a mighty promise to those who can occupy and wait until he comes.

**ESTHER**

*But they that wait upon the LORD shall renew their strength; they shall mount up with wings as eagles; they shall run, and not be weary; and they shall walk, and not faint.*

Isaiah 40:31

## • <u>OPERATE IN THE ANOINTING:</u>

It is extremely important to operate in the anointing. When you are plugged in to the source (JESUS) He can bring peace out of confusion, make the crooked ways straight and cause you to walk on water. Please don't prostitute God by using him just to bail you out when you are in over your head. There will be times in your life, like Esther, when you find yourself between the proverbial rock and the hard place and you need King Jesus on your bond. If you are truly abiding in him and have his word abiding in you, the gates of hell will not be able to prevail against you. Satan will huff and puff but he will never blow your house down because you operate in the anointing and the anointing will destroy every yoke. When you operate in the anointing, even your problems have to bow down and obey God's rules and limitations!!

*27And it shall come to pass in that day, that his burden shall be taken away from off thy shoulder, and his yoke from off thy neck, and the yoke shall be destroyed because of the anointing.*

Isaiah 10:27

# MY PERSONAL *HER*STORY PAGE

# **BOLDNESS**

> *"When you operate in the anointing, even your problems have to bow down and obey God's rules and limitations!!"*

**What are some problem areas in your life right now? List them below and lay them at the feet of Jesus.**

_____

_____

_____

_____

_____

_____

_____

_____

_____

## CHAPTER FIVE

# *FIVE WISE VIRGINS*

**CHARACTER TRAIT: WISDOM** (the quality or state of being wise; knowledge of what is true or right coupled with just judgment as to action; sagacity, discernment, or insight.)

## BACKGROUND SCRIPTURE: MATTHEW 25:1-10

*Then shall the kingdom of heaven be likened unto ten virgins, which took their lamps, and went forth to meet the bridegroom. And five of them were wise, and five were foolish. They that were foolish took their lamps, and took no oil with them: But the wise took oil in their vessels with their lamps. While the bridegroom tarried, they all slumbered and slept. And at midnight there was a cry made, Behold, the bridegroom cometh; go ye out to meet him. Then all those virgins arose, and trimmed their lamps. And the foolish said unto the wise, Give us of your oil; for our lamps are gone out. But the wise answered, saying, Not so; lest there be not enough for us and you: but go ye rather to them that sell, and buy for yourselves. And while they went to buy, the bridegroom came; and they that were ready went in with him to the marriage: and the door was shut. Afterward came also the*

# HERSTORY

**IF YOU DON'T LEARN FROM HERSTORY, YOU'RE DESTINED TO REPEAT IT!**

*other virgins, saying, Lord, Lord, open to us. But he answered and said, Verily I say unto you, I know you not. Watch therefore, for ye know neither the day nor the hour wherein the Son of man cometh.*

**HISTORY:** These five women are contrasted in Jesus' parable to illustrate the truth that just being a good church member and being part of the church is not enough. This parable shows what happens without warning when ten virgins were gathered with their lamps in the right place waiting for the bridegroom to come. Only five of the virgins had the wisdom to bring additional oil for their lamps in case the bridegroom was late or delayed. When He arrived, the five foolish virgins who didn't have oil were left out because they had left and were out trying to find oil for their vessels. By the time they made it back, they were locked out and the bridegroom solemnly declared, "I do not know you!"

## HERSTORY: RUNNING ON FUMES

Have there been times when you have felt burned out, stressed out, let down, put down, headed for a breakdown and a meltdown, because you were overloaded, heavy-loaded and burdened down with the cares of this world. In retrospect, is it possible that you, like the five foolish virgins, were running on fumes instead of casting all of my cares upon Jesus?

**Casting all your care upon him; for he careth for you.**

1 Peter 5:7

**FIVE WISE VIRGINS**

Let us carefully walk together through a five-part checklist that I've created and given the acronym of **F-U-M-E-S**. I will share five areas that can cause you (regardless of title, church affiliation, religious training, attendance schedule or ministry gift) to experience a spiritual meltdown and ultimately have the plug pulled on your God-given destiny. Take out a spiritual mirror or measuring stick and see how full your vessel is with the oil of the Holy Spirit. Are you running on F-U-M-E-S?

***F*—FLESH**—You cannot operate in the flesh and please God. The flesh warreth against the spirit and you must die daily to the flesh because in the flesh there is no good thing. If you try to deal with the everyday, mundane, routine tasks of life without the supernatural indwelling of the Holy Spirit, you will wear yourself down. The oil of the Holy Spirit is like natural oil. Oil is defined as any greasy substance that does not dissolve in water. Oils are classified as animal, mineral or vegetable and keeps things moist and moving. The oil of the Holy Spirit will keep you from rusting out and will keep you on the move for God.

Oil protects the inner parts, prevents friction and takes the heat out of Satan's fiery darts. There is no way to fight Satan in the natural.

***For we wrestle not against flesh and blood, but against principalities, against powers, against the rulers of the darkness of this world, against spiritual wickedness in high places.***

Ephesians 6:12

**HER**STORY  IF YOU DON'T LEARN FROM *HER*STORY, YOU'RE DESTINED TO REPEAT IT!

## U—USED TO BE, USED TO HAVE, USED TO FEEL:

So many saints are being defeated because they are relying on yesterday's power, yesterday's anointing, yesterday's sermon, or some other past spiritual victory. Just as you must die daily to self, you must be renewed on a daily basis. His mercies are renewed fresh every morning. Each new day, Satan will confront you with an old trick wrapped in a beautiful, new wrapper. It may look pretty, but his ultimate goal is to kill, steal and destroy. You must remember that he is already a defeated foe and misery loves company. His greatest enemy is Christ and you are Christ's greatest treasure. He treasured you so much that he laid down his life for you and me. To keep your oil burning fresh and plentiful, you must read the engrafted Word of God and meditate on His precepts, promises and principles each new day. Don't forget to read the meditation scriptures provided in the back of this book.

*But his delight is in the law of the LORD; and in his law doth he meditate day and night.*

Psalms 1:1

## M-MAN'S APPROVAL:

Some of you must check with your prayer partner, girlfriend, relative, co-worker or other trusted confidant before you do ANYTHING. Should I jump on one foot or two feet? Which route should I take to the mall? Should I get a manicure, pedicure or both today? Come on now! Get a grip. Proverbs 3:6 reminds us that we are to acknowledge the Lord in all of our ways. There is a way that may seem right unto a man, but the end thereof are the ways of death. God's eyes are in every place beholding the evil and the good. He will lead and guide you when you learn to ask God instead of man. The bible tells us that a sheep knows His voice. It is when we take time to speak with and quietly listen and obey Jesus' voice that he will direct us daily, dozens of time a day. He is very concerned about the minutia or minor details of our lives. If God says it, that settles it whether another person approves or not.

**In all thy ways acknowledge him, and he shall direct thy paths.**

Proverbs 3:6

**E—EMOTIONS**—We must learn to do the right thing regardless of how it feels. No doubt the five wise virgins did not feel like lugging a cumbersome container of extra oil. They wanted to be footloose and fancy-free like the five foolish virgins. They were wise enough to realize that some things are a short-term pain for a long-term gain. If I went by feelings, I would not have written the first line of this book. God assigned me the task of writing a book to help women who may be on pause like Lot's wife or may be ready to pull their own life support plug and throw in the towel. Don't do it! Please, don't pull the plug. Don't let your emotions control you. Find scriptures that parallel your problem or situation, anchor down with your bible, decree victory and watch God show up and show out.

## S—SOMEBODY ELSE'S OIL (LEARN TO SAY 'NO')

You must learn how to say "NO" to oil drainers. You can often tell the oil drainers in the church who are running on empty or even worse on **F-U-M-E-S** because:

- Without oil they are not able to be a light to a lost and perverse generation

- They have no energy or strength and will yield to the slightest provocation, temptation or test.

- They are the people talking the loudest, protesting loudest against the 'system' and operation of the church but doing the least to build it up. Remember that even a car will start screeching when it runs out of oil.

- Most importantly, without their own oil, they cannot maintain the fire that Jeremiah spoke of feeling even down to the bone level.


Remember the third chapter of Matthew speaks of being baptized with the Holy Ghost and with fire! Have you been baptized with the Holy Ghost and with fire? What are you waiting for? Have you been running on F-U-M-E-S?

**FIVE WISE VIRGINS**

*And when the day of Pentecost was fully come, they were all with one accord in one place. And suddenly there came a sound from heaven as of a rushing mighty wind, and it filled all the house where they were sitting. And there appeared unto them cloven tongues like as of fire, and it sat upon each of them.*

Acts 2:1-3

*I indeed baptize you with water unto repentance. but he that cometh after me is mightier than I, whose shoes I am not worthy to bear: he shall baptize you with the Holy Ghost, and with fire.*
**Matthew 3:11**

*Then I said, I will not make mention of him, nor speak any more in his name. But his word was in mine heart as a burning fire shut up in my bones, and I was weary with forbearing, and I could not stay*

Jeremiah 20:9

MY PERSONAL **HER**STORY PAGE

# **WISDOM**

> "You must learn how to say "no" to oil drainers."

**What are some the oil drainers in your life (People or things that stress you out and constantly drain you but yet have nothing to deposit into your life)?**

_____

_____

_____

_____

_____

_____

_____

_____

# CHAPTER SIX

# *HANNAH*

**CHARACTER TRAIT: HOPE** (the feeling that what is wanted can be had or that events will turn out for the best.)

**BACKGROUND SCRIPTURE:**

**1 Samuel 1:2** *And he had two wives; the name of the one was Hannah, and the name of the other Peninnah: and Peninnah had children, but Hannah had no children.*

**HISTORY:** Hannah was one of Elkanah's two wives and was the one most favored. Peninnah, his other wife and mother of his children, teased and taunted her for being barren and unable to bring forth fruit. She prayed in a spirit of travail and sincerity to God and vowed that if He would give her a son, she would give him to the Lord for service all of his life and would not cut his hair. After the priest acknowledged and granted her request, she returned home and bears Elkanah a son and named him Samuel. After she weaned him, she took him to the temple for Eli to use in the service of the Lord. She also was the mother of three more sons and two daughters.

# HERSTORY

IF YOU DON'T LEARN FROM *HER*STORY, YOU'RE DESTINED TO REPEAT IT!

## HERSTORY: WHAT IS YOUR DUE DATE?

Apostle Paul reminds us in the book of Galatians that we don't have to be weary in well doing. We are promised a due season or due date if we faint not. I'm sure that you have had seasons in your own life when it seemed that you were unable to 'birth' the ministry, dream, vision, relationship or success that God has ordained in your life.

***And let us not be weary in well doing: for in due season we shall reap, if we faint not.***

Galatians 6:9

After reading of Hannah's difficulty in bearing a child for her beloved husband, I was reminded of my

*Krystal and Kadriane sharing a special moment.*

own pregnancies and subsequent births of my two daughters. You too may be a mother, godmother, foster mother, grandmother or mother of an adopted child and recall the euphoria of holding that sweet little bundle of love in your arms after a fresh bath and a hefty sprinkling of baby powder and slathering of baby lotion. The coos and gurgles were music to your ears as your child snuggled in the warmth and security of your arms, comforted by the rhythmic beat of your love-filled heart.

Wow! It doesn't get too much better than this---the birth of a child. A child's birth can be symbolic of the cycle that often accompanies the birth of a dream, ministry or other desired goal.

Deuteronomy 11:13-14 outlines the prerequisites necessary to step into the due season in which your spirit has been impregnated. The online dictionary, www.dictionary.com defines pregnancy as 'the period from conception to birth when a woman carries a developing fetus in her uterus.' As many of you know and may have actually experienced, many things can go wrong during this period from conception to actual delivery of a baby. The same is true when birthing in the spiritual realm. Let us look at several mandates necessary for a healthy delivery with Dr. Jesus as your OBY-GYN and the Holy Spirit as your midwife!

**And it shall come to pass, if ye shall hearken diligently unto my commandments which I command you this day, to love the LORD your God, and to serve him with all your heart and with all**

# HERSTORY

IF YOU DON'T LEARN FROM HERSTORY, YOU'RE DESTINED TO REPEAT IT!

**your soul, That I will give you the rain of your land in his due season, the first rain and the latter rain, that thou mayest gather in thy corn, and thy wine, and thine oil.**

Deuteronomy 11:13-14

## EXAMINE YOURSELF:

The book of 2 Corinthians tells us to examine and prove ourselves regarding our faith walk. One of the first things that a woman needs during her prenatal care is a thorough examination from a competent obstetrician. This medical professional can be a valuable resource to the expectant mother in areas of diet, physical changes occurring in her body and most importantly her projected due date. I am the proud mother of two adult daughters and both came within a few days of their due date.

I can still remember being in labor and being driven to the hospital by my husband (now ex-husband) and the father of my daughters. As he drove me to Jackson Hospital, with my contractions coming less than five minutes apart, I noticed that he had suddenly become very sullen and quiet. I asked him what was wrong and he replied that he was not ready to have a baby now. He said that he was not ready to be a father, parked the car, signed me in at the front desk and said that he needed some 'rest'. He drove away nonchalantly as my labor pains intensified.

Fortunately, my mother had also come along in

the car and was proud to stay with me during this new experience that I was about to encounter. I still remember the warm compresses she put to my aching back and her gentle words of reassurance. Well, as it turned out, the contractions were real, and it was indeed my due date. Our daughter, Krystal, entered this world about 30 minutes before my husband returned from his nap.

When it's your due date, you can hold your breath, clap your hands, or sing your favorite hymn and it will not stop the imminent birth. The same concept is true when God has planted a seed in you. If it's of the Lord, you can't overthrow it. The very gates of Hell will not be able to prevail against you. What God has for you, it IS for you.

**And let us not be weary in well doing: for in due season we shall reap, if we faint not.**

Galatians 6:9

**And I say also unto thee, That thou art Peter, and upon this rock I will build my church; and the gates of hell shall not prevail against it.**

Matthew 16:18

It can be very difficult to maintain your focus and patience after God has impregnated you with an assignment, mission, ministry, idea, or dream because often God is the only one that knows the exact due date. You can labor and work for years and it seems that you fail to bring forth the fruit that God has promised. Have you examined yourself? Every good idea is NOT a God-idea. You can feel that something is so right and it can be so wrong—due to the wrong motive, the wrong season or involvement of the wrong people.

The bible itself offers the best ultrasound to use when checking to see that you are indeed carrying a seed of excellence that will bring honor and glory to God the father and that will help you to fulfill the great commission.

***Go ye therefore, and teach all nations, baptizing them in the name of the Father, and of the Son, and of the Holy Ghost:***

Matthew 28:19

***Examine yourselves, whether ye be in the faith; prove your own selves. Know ye not your own selves, how that Jesus Christ is in you, except ye be reprobates.***

2 Corinthians 13:5

## **MAKE SURE IT'S NOT A FALSE PREGNANCY:**

A thorough examination will verify that you are pregnant for real and not merely experiencing a false pregnancy. Your symptoms can be real—morning sickness, swollen feet, late night cravings, backaches, and even a noticeable increase in your abdominal girth. Upon a closer examination, however, even though you have all of the above symptoms, there is no fetal heartbeat. A close friend of my sister's had a false pregnancy that lasted about five months before she finally went in for a checkup, decked down in her new maternity frock only to be told by the doctor that the pregnancy was just a figment of her imagination. She went into a severe depression and almost lost her mind grieving over the loss of her imaginary child. She became a recluse for about a year and after much intercessory prayer and travail was finally able to face her church family and friends and get on with her life. To this very day, she refuses to discuss it.

This pathetic story of one woman, still barren to this very day, magnifies the importance of making sure that you have indeed heard the voice of God in whatever you do. The Holy Spirit must over shadow you like he did Mary, the mother of Jesus, impregnating you with the critical power, anointing, vision, and wisdom, that you need to give birth to the gifts, talents and assignments that he has placed in you.

## **DON'T MISCARRY:**

Doubting is one of the main emotions that Satan will use against you to make you miscarry you spiritual "baby". Learn to speak positively about the thing that God is trying to birth through you. Doubt can be in your mind but it's not unbelief until you speak it. You have the right to remain silent because anything you say can be used against you in the spiritual realm. Remember that death and life are in the power of the tongue. Satan wants to kill, steal and destroy the good thing that God has planned for you before the foundation of the world.

**Death *and* life *are in the power of the tongue: and they that love it shall eat the fruit thereof***

Proverbs 18:21

*The thief cometh not, but for to **steal**, **and** to **kill**, **and** to **destroy**: I am come that they might have life, and that they might have it more abundantly.*

St. John 10:10

## **DON'T LET THE ENEMY INDUCE LABOR:**

Your steps (due date) are ordered by the Lord and in due season, like Hannah, he will give you the desires of your heart. God's people are in such a hurry to go somewhere and oftentimes they don't even know where they are going. When they get there, they might meet themselves coming back. If Satan can't slow you down, he will most certainly cause you to fast-forward ahead without the backing, anointing or leading of the Holy Ghost.

The third chapter of Ecclesiastes tells us that there is a season for everything. If we operate out of season, it could be as disastrous as inducing labor during the first trimester of pregnancy or going sky- diving a week before your due date.

It is imperative that you allow God to order you steps.

**HANNAH**

Your role is just to flow with him and be led by His quiet still voice. If you try to elevate yourself, toot your own horn or operate in an area of ministry that God has not totally groomed you for, the 'baby' might not survive.

Don't let a well-meaning prayer partner, or false prophet induce your labor before time. You shall reap in due season if you faint not.

## DON'T BE ALARMED WHEN YOUR WATER BREAKS:

One of my friends, in the final phase of her third trimester, was in the grocery store when her water broke. To avoid being discovered and ultimately embarrassed, she grabbed a jar of pickles and dropped it on the floor cleverly diverting attention from herself to the messy puddle. She had been experiencing mild labor pains all day, but once her water broke, the severity of the pains almost tripled.

It was her third child and about an hour after arriving at the hospital, her beautiful, healthy son was born.

In the spiritual realm, when your water breaks (attacks from the enemy that brings tears of **water**), be encouraged and don't despair because the birth is VERY, VERY near!!!

**Wherefore take unto you the whole armour of God, that ye may be able to withstand in the evil day, and having done all, to stand.**

Ephesians 6:13

**HER**STORY   IF YOU DON'T LEARN FROM **HER**STORY, YOU'RE DESTINED TO REPEAT IT!

## FINALLY:

**P** ---PRAY

**U** ---UNTIL

**S** ---SOMETHING

**H** ---HAPPENS

MY PERSONAL *HER*STORY PAGE

# *HOPE*

> " Remember that death and life are in the power of the tongue."

**Make a list of 10 positive affirmations that you will speak over your life and situation each day. (Example: I will maintain a pleasant attitude today and refuse to be negatively influenced by others):**

_____

_____

_____

_____

_____

_____

_____

_____

_____

_____

# CHAPTER SEVEN

## JOB'S WIFE

**CHARACTER TRAIT: ANGER** (a strong feeling of displeasure or belligerence)

**BACKGROUND SCRIPTURE:**

*Again there was a day when the sons of God came to present themselves before the LORD, and Satan came also among them to present himself before the LORD. And the LORD said unto Satan, From whence comest thou? And Satan answered the LORD, and said, From going to and fro in the earth, and from walking up and down in it. And the LORD said unto Satan, Hast thou considered my servant Job, that there is none like him in the earth, a perfect and an upright man, one that feareth God, and escheweth evil? and still he holdeth fast his integrity, although thou movedst me against him, to destroy him without cause. And Satan answered the LORD, and said, Skin for skin, yea, all that a man hath will he give for his life. But put forth thine hand now, and touch his bone and his flesh, and he will curse thee to thy face. And the LORD said unto Satan, Behold, he is in thine hand; but save his life. So went Satan forth from the presence of the LORD, and smote Job with*

# HERSTORY

IF YOU DON'T LEARN FROM HERSTORY, YOU'RE DESTINED TO REPEAT IT!

*sore boils from the sole of his foot unto his crown. And he took him a potsherd to scrape himself withal; and he sat down among the ashes. Then said his wife unto him, Dost thou still retain thine integrity? curse God, and die. But he said unto her, Thou speakest as one of the foolish women speaketh. What? shall we receive good at the hand of God, and shall we not receive evil? In all this did not Job sin with his lips.*

Job 2:1-10

**HISTORY:** Mrs. Job was the mother of Job's three daughters and seven sons and was able to hold her peace when they loss all of their children and wealth in a single day. However, when Satan, in his second test, attacked Job with painful, stinking ulcers from his head to his toes, she couldn't hold her peace and cried out, **"Curse God and die!"** She didn't divorce Job, but claimed that she was repulsed by even the smell of his breath. After his divine healing, she bore three more daughters and seven more sons for him.

## HERSTORY: LET THE LORD BUILD YOUR HOUSE

**"Except the Lord build the house, they labor in vain that build it; except the Lord keep the city, the watchman waketh but in vain."**

Psalms 127:1

Mrs. Job was probably no different than many of you. No doubt she had high hopes, and starry-eyed dreams of living happily ever after with the love of her life. She had waited for years and finally, God had allowed her to raise her ten beautiful children to adulthood. "Wow!" She probably thought, "This is the life. I'm living comfortable as I tiptoe through the tulips of life, smelling the roses and adjusting to being an empty nester. My kids are out of the house now so Job and I can sleep late, go for long walks, work out together, and even go to our little, secret get-a-way once in a while."

She soon learned that Job constantly worried about his children and made sacrifices on their behalf in case they had sinned. This became a constant obsession for him and ultimately his greatest fear. Satan capitalized on his fear and used it as an entry point to attack the family and 'house' (earthly tabernacle) of this perfect and upright man.

Soon, her joy and hope turned to bitterness and anger. Have the trials and tests in your life made you bitter or better? When a lump of clay is placed in the sun it hardens, while a lump of wax will soften. How will you respond to life's inevitable disappointments, letdowns, put-downs, setbacks and surprises? How will the next chapter of your life story read?

**For God hath not given us the spirit of fear; but of power, and of love, and of a sound mind**

2 Timothy 1:7

# HERSTORY

*IF YOU DON'T LEARN FROM HERSTORY, YOU'RE DESTINED TO REPEAT IT!*

**The steps of a good man are ordered by the LORD: and he delighteth in his way.**

Psalms 37:23

**Neither gives place to the devil.**

Ephesians 4:27

In order to fully understand the destructive force of anger, let's look at possible entry points that Satan tries to use to destroy your spiritual house. He almost succeeded in destroying the home of Mr. and Mrs. Job through her angry tantrum. We will use the different phases in the construction of a natural house to illustrate the different stages that Satan can enter and wreck havoc. You'll see that there is no need to get angry about the hand that has been dealt to you. I believe that God has planted a seed of excellence in you that will ultimately triumph if you don't let the weeds of bitterness and anger choke it out.

**BLUEPRINT:** The bible is the best blueprint to use for success because man cannot live by bread alone, but by every word that proceeds out of the mouth of God. Find out what God's word says about something before you speak it or do it. It can revolutionize your life.

Like Job and Mrs. Job, Satan had drafted a counterfeit blueprint for my life before I was even born. My first concrete memory of myself was around the age of four picking up pecans one cold winter morning in

**JOB'S WIFE**

the country town of Greenwood (about an hour's drive west of Tallahassee, Florida.)

Although I didn't realize it at the time, I was born in abject poverty and raised by my single mother and grandmother in a small community dissected by dusty dirt roads without names or streetlights. I had to walk about a mile to catch the school bus for the first 6 years of school while dodging the neighbor's bulldogs and being scared speechless by the many varieties of snakes that slithered near our route. I should have been excited when our road was finally added to the bus route, but I was actually embarrassed because

*This is the house that the author was born in. Notice the field rocks supporting the house.*

# HER STORY

**IF YOU DON'T LEARN FROM HER STORY, YOU'RE DESTINED TO REPEAT IT!**

our house was a two-bedroom shack that had never been painted. It was held up by mix-matched field rocks and surrounded by old, moss-covered pecan trees. I can still remember the roar of laughter and the painful jeering that my sisters and I endured the first afternoon that the bus driver put us off, shifted into drive and sped off into the sunset with the other students. We were one of the families that the poor people called "po".

We gathered pecans to earn money for the county fair but often didn't get to go because we didn't have transportation. We often went on the back of *Mr. Sam Gray's pick-up truck. Our embarrassment soon melted away as we entered the world of coin tosses, two-headed roosters, merry-go-rounds, corn dogs, cotton candy, candied apples and the tattooed carnival workers.

My mother supported us with income from her job as a maid in the homes of some of the more affluent families located in nearby Marianna. My older sister Mattie would occasionally send ten or twenty dollars to help supplement my mother's income. I saw my first hundred-dollar bill when Mattie sent it in a letter to our mom to help out with Christmas presents. She was a young college student herself, who had recently relocated to Rochester, New York, but managed to siphon off some of her financial aid money to help her struggling family back home.

Since we never owned a car, my mother had to carpool with five other workers in a car without seat

## JOB'S WIFE

belts. They were packed in that car like a bunch of sardines. *Mr. Sampson Reed came around 5:30 in the morning to pick her up and we often didn't see her again until around 6:00 in the evening.

She was (and still is) a wonderful mother and constantly encouraged us to 'rank up' so that we could make something out of ourselves. She instilled an intense desire in me to rewrite my life story and leave that life of poverty and lack. I went on to graduate second in my class from high school, attended community college in Marianna and attended graduate and undergraduate schools at Florida State University. I had to live in the dorm all of my college life because I did not have my own car. I had to catch the campus bus or walk to class because it was a long way from Sally Hall to my classes at the Regional Rehab Center on FSU campus. I almost froze at the bus stop and almost died of asthma because I tried to dress cute instead of warm. Fortunately, I know better now!

I am currently enjoying a wonderful career as a speech pathologist working with students who have articulation, voice, fluency, language or reading disorders. I have had the honor of teaching students from Pre-K to college and have learned many lessons from them as well. I have also taught Public Speaking and Fundamentals of Interpersonal Communications at Tallahassee Community College and loved it.

I've been blessed with wonderful students, parents, admini-strators, and co-workers along the way.

# HER STORY

**IF YOU DON'T LEARN FROM HERSTORY, YOU'RE DESTINED TO REPEAT IT!**

I am the pastor of a loving, growing church in Tallahassee, Florida and thoroughly enjoy my role as pastor. I feel so blessed and highly favored to be able to serve a group of sincere, motivated members who too have stories of trial and triumph. Everybody has a story to tell. I am humbled by this opportunity to tell my story along with the women from Genesis to Revelation.

As you see, the blueprint has been altered. The Lord flipped the script in my life and He can do the same for you. My early life of poverty was just one small chapter in my **HER**story book, but thank God it wasn't the end of the story. I refused to let anger keep me from pressing on in spite of difficulty.

Job's wife thought that she would never be able to be intimate and enjoy her husband's loving embrace again. She avoided his offensive breath and fed him out of a long-handled spoon when he tried to rekindle the fire. Nevertheless, she learned the hard way that God, in due season, will alter situations and circumstances just for you. He can and will restore everything that the enemy has destroyed or taken away from you. Mrs. Job's anger and bitterness could have resulted in the loss of their marriage and possibly their lives. Bitterness is like lye or acid—it destroys the container that it's stored in as well as the materials that it contacts. Anger is self-destructive and caustic.

**THE BUILDING PERMIT:** I have learned that Satan can't touch you without God's permission. He must apply for a permit to even touch your spiritual building. He must get permission from God because your life is hid with Christ with God. It is so well hidden that Satan can't even find you. He may aim his fiery darts at you but will miss every time! Halleluiah!

Don't get angry with God! Recognize that God does nothing bad to you. He doesn't make you sick or diseased. He doesn't make you lose your job, best friend or husband. He's not the one to blame when your house was damaged in the storm or your new SUV totaled. Satan is behind every bad thing that happens in your life. He cannot launch an attack at all without God's knowledge, permission and ultimate resolution and deliverance.

**For ye are dead, and your life is hid with Christ in God.**

Colossians 3:3

**There hath no temptation taken you but such as is common to man: but God is faithful, who will not suffer you to be tempted above that ye are able; but will with the temptation also make a way to escape, that ye may be able to bear it.**

1 Corinthians 10:13

**THE FOUNDATION:** God's word is settled in heaven. When you build your life and dreams on God's Word, this represents a solid foundation that will last throughout eternity. Friendships will fail. Treaties will terminate. Marriages will dissolve. Business deals will fizzle out, but his Word abides forever. If you sell out to the Lord Jesus Christ and stand on His Word, you will not get angry when Satan tries to bait you through adversity, trials or temptations. Instead, you must purpose in your heart not to take the 'bait'. Remember a fish won't get caught if he keeps his mouth shut. Don't let your mouth cause you to lose a blessing or charge God foolishly. Memorize the scriptures located in the back of this book and when Satan comes in like a flood, the Spirit of the Lord will lift up a standard against him.

***For verily I say unto you, Till heaven and earth pass, one jot or one tittle shall in no wise pass from the law, till all be fulfilled.***

Matthew 5:18

**THE FRAME:** You must remember that you are merely dust and that in Jesus; you live move and have your very being. Since He knew you before you were in your mother's womb, He is the one that can repair, knit together, soothe, renew, relieve, calm, stabilize, regulate, strengthen, revive, and ultimately heal your body from head to toe and from the inside out.

Our family could have easily allowed ourselves to become angry with God when once again he pulled back the hedge and allowed Satan to viciously attack another one of our loved ones. This time it was Mom. One of the many rattlesnakes that slithered freely through the wooded terrain of our neighborhood bit my mother on the ankle one cool December morning causing her to almost lose her entire leg as well as her life. She was simply raking leaves in her front yard when the thing that she feared most came upon her.

After she realized that she had been bitten, she went in the house, tied a homemade cord around her leg, called the hospital and attempted to drive herself to the hospital. Thankfully, she didn't have to drive herself and accepted the kind offer of her neighbor and family friend, *Mrs. Sandy Brown. After arriving at the hospital, we soon discovered that she was allergic to the anti-venom formula and had to be treated with high doses of antibiotics. The doctors were not sure that the antibiotics would work but once again, God thwarted Satan's attack on one of his servants, and three weeks later, she was released from the hospital as good as new. I know that it was God who allowed the antibiotics to work because He works with medical science. If we had allowed bitterness and anger to set in, it would have cancelled out the positive effect of the prayers.

Anger is related to fear and we know that God has not given us a spirit of fear. Oftentimes, people are angry because they are afraid. Mrs. Job may have been afraid or imagined that Job would become an invalid and wasn't sure if she would be able to care for him properly. You must cast down imaginations and strongholds and then stand back and see the salvation of the Lord. Don't let your mind play tricks on you.

# HERSTORY
**IF YOU DON'T LEARN FROM HERSTORY, YOU'RE DESTINED TO REPEAT IT!**

**Casting down *imaginations, and every high thing that exalteth itself against the knowledge of God, and bringing into captivity every thought to the obedience of Christ;***

2 Corinthians 10:5

Remember that Dr. Jesus makes house calls! According to Revelations 3:20, he will abide or live inside of you if you just open up and let him in. When Satan tries to huff and puff and blow your house down, the Lord himself will lift up a standard against him. Satan will try to bait you with things to make you worry and despair but DON'T TAKE THE BAIT. His bark is far worse than his bite. God sees the greatness in you when Satan calls you garbage, Jesus sees the treasure in you when the world calls you trash and yes, Jesus will pick you up if He has to reach WAY down. The Lord knows our frame and he will strengthen us if we acknowledge him and rest in him.

***So shall they fear the name of the LORD from the west, and his glory from the rising of the sun. When the enemy shall come in like a flood, the Spirit of the LORD shall lift up a standard against him.***

Isaiah 59:19

MY PERSONAL *HER*STORY PAGE

# ANGER

> *"God has planted a seed of excellence in you that will ultimately triumph if you don't let the weeds of bitterness and anger choke it out."*

**List the things and people that have caused you to feel angry within the last month. Write them below and then release them to the Lord.**

_____
_____
_____
_____
_____
_____
_____
_____
_____
_____

# CHAPTER EIGHT

# JABEZ'S MOTHER

**CHARACTER TRAIT: DESPAIR** (to lose, give up, or be without hope)

**BACKGROUND SCRIPTURE:**

*And Jabez was more honourable than his brethren: and his mother called his name Jabez, saying, Because I bare him with sorrow. And Jabez called on the God of Israel, saying, Oh that thou wouldest bless me indeed, and enlarge my coast, and that thine hand might be with me, and that thou wouldest keep me from evil, that it may not grieve me! And God granted him that which he requested.*

HISTORY: This mother named her son Jabez (which means **pain or distress**) because she bore him in pain. Even though Jabez was given a name with such negative connotations, he prayed himself that the Lord would change the significance of his name and give him joy instead of distress and peace instead of pain.

1 Chronicles 4:9-10

# HERSTORY

IF YOU DON'T LEARN FROM HERSTORY, YOU'RE DESTINED TO REPEAT IT!

## HERSTORY:

The chronology of Jabez's mother's pregnancy does not allow bible readers a behind-the-scenes glimpse into the horrific post-partum depression that caused her to give him a name synonymous with doom and gloom. We do know that it was a despair so overwhelming and consuming that she gave him a name that could have potentially labeled him for the rest of his life. Was Jabez a product of a date rape or incest? Had her husband or illicit lover walked off and left her in the weeks prior to her due date? What caused this mother to throw in the towel and give up on her newborn son? In this brief commentary, we will focus primarily on Jabez instead of his mother. It was important to set the stage of his mother's despair and hopelessness to show how Jabez was able to implement a 'Plan "B" and avoid the sad prophetic future that his name symbolized.

No doubt you too have been called everything but a child of God. There may have been names spoken or called over your life: SLOB, LAZY, FAT, STUPID, DEADBEAT, SICKLY, POOR, and the list goes on and on.

Jabez soon learned that his name was different and the school children probably taunted him mercilessly. He was sick and tired of being teased, humiliated, treated like a second-class citizen and discriminated against. He was tired of his schoolmates calling him names like 'Jay Bee'. Suddenly, something rose up within him that sparked a glimmer of hope in his spirit.

**JABEZ'S MOTHER**

Jabez decided within his spirit to shut out the world and cry out to God—he got serious with God and decided to FLIP THE SCRIPT! He needed a PLAN "**B**". It was the end of one chapter but it was certainly not the end of the book.

In other words, he knew that Satan's ultimate plan was to kill, steal and destroy him, but God always has a "PLAN B". God has a PLAN "B" for our lives also. According to **I Corinthians 2:9**, it has not even 'entered into our hearts the things which God hath prepared for them that love him'. If you are going through a dark period in your life and feel that you are at the end of your rope with no hope, remember that there is always a PLAN "B". Set the record straight: Your bush may be on fire but it does not have to burn up!

**But as it is written, Eye hath not seen, nor ear heard, neither have entered into the heart of man, the things which God hath prepared for them that love him.**

1 Corinthians 2:9

**Let's take a look at the MASTER PLAN, THE GAME PLAN and the LAY-A-WAY PLAN—three major components of PLAN "B".**

**MASTER PLAN:** In going back to Genesis, we see that Adam and Eve had it made in the shade---peace, security, unity, love, provision, health, pain-free and the list goes on and on. Because of the disobedience and ultimate fall of Adam and Eve, man could not live out God's original or MASTER PLAN. He sent his son Jesus as a "PLAN "B" when his original plan was foiled. He loved us too much to leave us without a way to escape. According to 1 Corinthians 10:13, "There is no temptation taken you but such that is common to man, but God is faithful who will not suffer you to be tempted above that ye are able; but will with the temptation also make a way to escape that ye may be able to bear it." In other words, God always has a PLAN "B".

**GAME PLAN:** When faced with a bleak future or sudden attack from the enemy, we must be like Jabez and have a strategy or game plan in place that will guarantee victory. We must…………..

- Acknowledge the Lord in prayer and ask God to show us what's in our own heart. Sometimes the true cause of our physical, emotional or mental illness may be hardness of the attitude, or faintness of heart.

- Use the Word to fight the enemy and to remind God of his promises to us. PROCLAIM instead of COMPLAIN!!

Reach deep within God's Word to find deliverance from your sicknesses, problems, hang-ups, idiosyncrasies, and take your eyes off of people. There will even come a time when even your pastor or leader can't help you. When you find yourself between the proverbial rock and a hard place, T.D. might loose

*JABEZ'S MOTHER*

you, Juanita might take you behind the veil, and Benny might blow on you, but nobody can do you like JESUS!

- Close out distractions and hindrances from external sources, including people. Oftentimes, you worry about what people think about your situation instead of what the Word says about it.

**LAY-A-WAY PLAN:**

Jesus already paid the price for any situation that we cannot endure. When he laid down His life on Calvary, He said 'it is finished'. Jesus gave His life so that you could have another chance or (PLAN "B") which He calls abundant life in St. John 10:10. Jesus not only cares about **WHO** you are but who you can **BECOME**. He knows that you have a seed of excellence that God planted in you before you were in your mother's womb. Now is the time to pull out the engrafted word of God and start on PLAN "B" so that your seed of excellence will spring forth in fulfilling God's purpose.

Like Jabez, you will discover that it may be the end of the chapter but it is not the end of the book. God attended to Jabez and answered his prayers. <u>WHAT A MIGHTY GOD WE SERVE!!!</u>

MY PERSONAL **HER**STORY PAGE

# *DESPAIR*

> *"Your bush may be on fire but it does not have to burn up!"*

**What are the things in your life that you feel you have little or no control over? You have prayed and things remain the same. List them below:**

_____

_____

_____

_____

_____

_____

_____

_____

_____

# CHAPTER NINE

## *SAMARITAN WOMAN*

**CHARACTER TRAIT: ATONEMENT** (satisfaction or reparation for a wrong or injury)

**BACKGROUND SCRIPTURE:** St. John 7-30

*There cometh a woman of Samaria to draw water: Jesus saith unto her, Give me to drink. (For his disciples were gone away unto the city to buy meat.) Then saith the woman of Samaria unto him, How is it that thou, being a Jew, askest drink of me, which am a woman of Samaria? for the Jews have no dealings with the Samaritans. Jesus answered and said unto her, If thou knewest the gift of God, and who it is that saith to thee, Give me to drink; thou wouldest have asked of him, and he would have given thee living water. The woman saith unto him, Sir, thou hast nothing to draw with, and the well is deep: from whence then hast thou that living water? Art thou greater than our father Jacob, which gave us the well, and drank thereof himself, and his children, and his cattle? Jesus answered and said unto her, Whosoever drinketh of this water shall thirst again: But whosoever drinketh of the water that I shall give him shall never thirst; but the water that I shall give him*

# HERSTORY

**IF YOU DON'T LEARN FROM *HER*STORY, YOU'RE DESTINED TO REPEAT IT!**

shall be in him a well of water springing up into everlasting life. The woman saith unto him, Sir, give me this water, that I thirst not, neither come hither to draw. Jesus saith unto her, Go, call thy husband, and come hither. The woman answered and said, I have no husband. Jesus said unto her, Thou hast well said, I have no husband: For thou hast had five husbands; and he whom thou now hast is not thy husband: in that saidst thou truly. The woman saith unto him, Sir, I perceive that thou art a prophet. Our fathers worshipped in this mountain; and ye say, that in Jerusalem is the place where men ought to worship. Jesus saith unto her, Woman, believe me, the hour cometh, when ye shall neither in this mountain, nor yet at Jerusalem, worship the Father. Ye worship ye know not what: we know what we worship: for salvation is of the Jews. But the hour cometh, and now is, when the true worshippers shall worship the Father in spirit and in truth: for the Father seeketh such to worship him. God is a Spirit: and they that worship him must worship him in spirit and in truth. The woman saith unto him, I know that Messias cometh, which is called Christ: when he is come, he will tell us all things. Jesus saith unto her, I that speak unto thee am he. And upon this came his disciples, and marvelled that he talked with the woman: yet no man said, What seekest thou? or, Why talkest thou with her? The woman then left her waterpot, and went her way into the city, and saith to the men, Come, see a

**SAMARITAN WOMAN**

man, which told me all things that ever I did: is not this the Christ? Then they went out of the city, and came unto him.

**HISTORY:** Jesus was a Jew who had stopped in the town of Sychar in Samaria to get water and to get some rest. He had sent his disciples into town to get some food. The woman at the well was there around noontime to draw water as well. She felt uncomfortable with, Jesus, a Jew, asking her, a Samaritan for water because it was a forbidden act. The Samaritans were considered heretics and unclean. After dialoging for a few minutes, Jesus told her about her past even though this was their first encounter. He exposed the fact that she had had five husbands and the man she was currently living with was not even her husband. He revealed himself to her as the Son of God, the Messiah, as proven by his knowledge of her colorful past. She immediately dropped her water pots and ran back to the townsfolk encouraging them to "Come see a man".

**HERSTORY: LOOKING FOR LOVE IN ALL THE WRONG PLACES**

The woman at the well, commonly referred to as the Samaritan Woman, certainly had a very colorful life and quite a story to tell. Her only crime was that she looked for love in all the wrong places. She had tried to find the love of her life in the arms of her five husbands. She tried to do it the conventional way but failed miserably time and time again. She finally threw in the towel and decided to "shack" with her latest

# HERSTORY

*IF YOU DON'T LEARN FROM HERSTORY, YOU'RE DESTINED TO REPEAT IT!*

heart throb. She put her dreams and hopes on hold and just settled for a mediocre existence.

Some of you are like the Samaritan Woman, looking for natural sources to fulfill a divine need. There is a God-shaped vacuum in each of us that God has reserved just for Himself. The third chapter of Revelation reminds us of how much he wants to come in and sup with us and abide with us.

***Behold, I stand at the door, and knock: if any man hear my voice, and open the door, I will come in to him, and will sup with him, and he with me.***

Revelation 3:20

As a pastor, I have heard it all and have counseled dozens of women (I have counseled men also, but this is a book about **HER**story) with stories of abuse, betrayal, poverty, disappointment, loneliness, guilt, fear and desperation who are still trying to 'find' themselves. These women invariably fail to seek the Lord early in their careers, marriages, educational pursuits or other choices in life and end up never being the woman that God intended them to be. They end up going round and round the same mountains for years and never coming into the full knowledge of the truth.

Some of these women were near or at their breaking point by the time that they came for help. Little did they know that Jesus broke the laws of:

- **BIOLOGY**—He was born of a virgin.

**SAMARITAN WOMAN**

- **METEOROLGY**—He spoke to the wind.

- **PSYCHOLOGY**—He healed a demoniac in one session.

- **CHEMISTRY**-He turned water into wine.

- **PSYSIOLOGY**-He healed crippled bodies.

- **THEOLOGY**-He came not with enticing words of man's wisdom.

- **POVERTY**-He turned a fish mouth into an ATM machine.

- **GRAVITY**—He walked on water.

There is no situation or **HER**story that he has not heard and no sin so shameful that he can't forgive. God placed a seed of excellence in you before the foundation of the world even before you were in your mother's womb. God wants you to be your personal best—He sees the treasure in you when you feel like trash, the greatness in you when you're treated like garbage. He'll pick you up if he has to reach way down.

***I love them that love* me*; and those that seek* me *early* shall find me.**

Proverbs 8:17

Have you ever put a challenging puzzle together only to discover that there is one missing piece? Even though you were proud of your skill and perseverance,

# HERSTORY
**IF YOU DON'T LEARN FROM HERSTORY, YOU'RE DESTINED TO REPEAT IT!**

the loss of that one missing piece kept you from a total sense of accomplishment and total fulfillment. That puzzle piece is symbolic of the place in each of our hearts that God purposely left for Himself. He stands at the door ready to come into your hearts and heal you everywhere you hurt.

In your feeble attempt to deal with the loneliness, mask the pain, and silence the inner turmoil in your heart, you may try unsuccessfully to mask the pain, fit in with the clique or immerse yourself with the latest fad or cultural sensation. Some of you are trying to fill the void with a frenzy of church activity and programs. In one week you may try to squeeze in choir practice, revival services, bible study, intercessory prayer, vacation bible school (VBS), a Saturday morning women's conference, prayer breakfast plus a musical concert on Sunday night. You convince yourself that it is all a part of ministry and that you will be rewarded in that sweet by and by.

Just look around you and observe the tremendous amount of time and energy that some women put into trying to impress others and validate themselves while often ignoring God. My question to you is, "When do you find time to read your bible"? "When do you fast?" "Are you ever still and quiet enough to hear that soft, still voice of the Holy Spirit trying to minister to you?" "When did you take time to turn off the T.V. (Yes, even Christian T.V. and inspirational networks) and look into the eyes of your family members and actively listen to them?

## SAMARITAN WOMAN

Did you listen carefully without dividing your attention with a second or third project simultaneously (more commonly known as multi-tasking)?

As you may have already discovered, none of these things will mend a broken heart, heal you when you're sick or fill the God-shaped void in your heart. No amount of education, social status or man-designated titles can replace the place in your heart that God has reserved for Himself. He won't share this spot with anything or anyone else.

The woman at the well symbolizes every woman who's been put down, let down, cast aside, kicked to the curb, overlooked, overworked, lied on, or cheated on. She does not have a name like Abigail, Anna, Deborah, Esther, Hannah, or Sapphirra. She is merely referred to as 'the woman'. The Samaritan woman of 2007 could be the woman next door, the lady in the next cubicle at work, or even the lady in the mirror—**YOU**! What is your **HER**STORY?

The Samaritan Woman was glad to finally be able to come clean and 'fess up' to her years of man trouble, heartache and pain. She was shunned and ostracized by the other women in town and had a reputation that was less than favorable. She was in it by herself and felt so all alone. She came to the conclusion that she had nothing to **LOSE**, nothing to **HIDE** and nothing to **PROVE**. She risked all on a man from Galilee and tasted and saw that the Lord is good (Psalms 34:8). When Jesus shared with her a more excellent way, she dropped her water pots and shared the good news

# HERSTORY
**IF YOU DON'T LEARN FROM HERSTORY, YOU'RE DESTINED TO REPEAT IT!**

with others. We too have an obligation to share the good news about the atonement provided through the blood of Jesus! Tell someone your story today and use your personal **HER**story to encourage someone else to hold on!

***O taste and see that the LORD is good: blessed is the man that trusteth in him.***

Psalms 34:8

***And the LORD said unto Cain, Where is Abel thy brother? And he said, I know not: Am I my brother's keeper?***

Genesis 4:9

Yes! Indeed! We are our brother and sister's keeper.

MY PERSONAL *HER*STORY PAGE

## *ATONEMENT*

> *"When did you take time to turn off the T.V. (Yes, even Christian T.V. and inspirational networks) and look into the eyes of your family members and actively listen to them?*

**Please list below the family and friends that you need to take the time to connect with on this week.**

_____

_____

_____

_____

_____

_____

_____

_____

_____

_____

## CHAPTER TEN

# SAPPHIRA

**CHARACTER TRAIT: DISHONESTY** (lack of honesty; a disposition to lie, cheat, or steal)

**HISTORY:** Sapphira, Ananias's wife, was a member of the early Christian church. She along with her husband conspired to withhold a portion of the money that they received from the sale of property they had recently sold. They supposedly came willingly to turn the total amount over to the Apostles for the benefit of the community, but secretly withheld an undisclosed amount for some other use. Sapphira, along with her husband, fell dead at Peter's feet and was buried the same day causing fear and awe throughout the church. It was the Holy Ghost that revealed the true nature of their deceitful hearts.

**BACKGROUND SCRIPTURE:**

*But a certain man named Ananias, with Sapphira his wife, sold a possession, And kept back part of the price, his wife also being privy to it, and brought a certain part, and laid it at the apostles' feet. But Peter said, Ananias, why hath Satan filled thine heart to lie to the Holy Ghost, and to keep back part of the price of the land?* **Acts: 5:1-3**

# **HER**STORY  IF YOU DON'T LEARN FROM *HER*STORY, YOU'RE DESTINED TO REPEAT IT!

## **HER**STORY: LAY IT ON THE LINE

I'm sure that you can relate to Sister Sapphira and her 'bad choice'. No doubt the Holy Spirit had troubled her conscience and tried to sway her to do the right thing but the constant warring of her flesh and spirit became too intense. Perhaps she had filled out a tithe envelope with every intention of following through, but once again, the enemy tricked her into thinking she could actually lie to the Holy Ghost. Didn't she know that God's eyes are in every place beholding the good, the bad and the ugly?

***The eyes of the LORD are in every place, beholding the evil and the good.***

Proverbs 15:3

You too probably remember the embarrassment and shame of being caught 'with your hand in the cookie jar'. When caught red-handed, you may have played the blame game, pulled out the race card, or held a poor-little-me party before taking responsibility for your actions, repenting before God and if necessary making amends with your fellow man. Like Sapphira, you too have a story to tell—dust under the rug, skeletons in the closet, things from your past that you may not be proud of. There is a human tendency to blame someone or something like our first parents did in the Garden of Eden.

***And the man said, The woman whom thou gavest to be with me, she gave me of the tree, and I did***

**SAPPHIRA**

eat. And the LORD God said unto the woman, What is this that thou hast done? And the woman said, The serpent beguiled me, and I did eat

Genesis 3:12-13

Now, thousands of years later, God's precious creation is still making excuses and refusing to be honest and transparent with their maker—the one who knows them better than they know themselves. He is the lifter up of your heads, the one that can make the crooked ways straight and bring peace out of confusion. Why not come clean and lay it on the line.

Satan has drawn a line in the sand and wants you, like Sapphira to cross the line to flee dishonesty, deceit and lying. In this chapter, I will expose three spiritual 'lines' that you must cross over in the sands of time to ensure your victory and ultimate triumph over the enemy:

## 1.) THE SEPERATION LINE:

Once and for all, you must purpose in your heart that for God you will live and for God you'll die. You must 'get real' and climb off the fence of hypocrisy and sell out to God. Being sold out means that you decide to have a high standard of holiness according to God's Word. Develop a strong conviction that you will not take your hand off the gospel plow for popularity, fame or fortune or ANYBODY.

Even though I did not receive the Holy Ghost until I was in college, I was taught principles of Christian

# HER**STORY**   IF YOU DON'T LEARN FROM HER**STORY,** YOU'RE DESTINED TO REPEAT IT!

living at an early age. One of the main things that my mother harped on during my teen years was, "Mira, make sure that you don't let none of these little boys mess you up. Try to hold yourself up 'til you marry". I was able to keep this promise but had many opportunities to cross the line after being enticed and lured by many bible-toting, hymn singing deacons and ministers in our community—most of whom were already married.

I vividly recall going out when I was college student for a movie date with a seemingly nice young man. On the ride back, he took a back route and before I noticed, we were on a deserted, dirt road in the middle of nowhere. His Dr. Jekle and Mr. Clyde persona soon became apparent as he advised me to 'put out or get out'. Of course I refused and was promptly put out of the car in the middle of the 'boonies'. I was totally overwhelmed as I watched his tail lights grow dimmer and dimmer as he drove away. He was gone only a couple of minutes but it seemed like an eternity. He slowly backed the car up, said, "get in" and drove me to the dorm in silence.

I immediately called my mother and told her about my date from the 'lake' and audibly shaken, she asked me his name. After I revealed the name of the young man who had asked such an unfair question, she said, "Elmira, that's your brother." I was appalled! Another family secret! I was the last to know. We had many conversations about the details surrounding this family secret, which yielded hours of up-close-and-personal conversations between my mother and I. These interpersonal communications allowed me to get to know her hurts, her dreams, her failures, her choices and **HER**story while allowing me a rare opportunity to get to know her not only as a parent but also as a woman

I shall never forget the time that my mother invited the local pastor for a delicious dinner of succulent roast beef with carrots, white acre peas with steamed okra, sliced tomatoes, rice, blackberry doobie, and delicious, homemade lemonade. After I excused myself from the dining room table to go into the kitchen to begin washing dishes, I became acutely aware of someone standing behind me. I quickly turned around just in time to receive a stolen kiss from the pastor. I immediately pushed him away and he nonchalantly played it off saying, "May I have a cold drink of water please?" As I handed him the glass of water, he acted as if nothing had happened and walked briskly back into the dining room to join his wife and the other dinner guests. Needless to say, I never took any of his sermons seriously from that day to this. After I moved to Tallahassee to attend FSU, he would call the dorm begging to come down for a 'visit'. My answer was always "NO". I wasn't saved, but I knew it was wrong.

After I was saved and filled with the Holy Spirit , I was able to witness to him about true holiness. He stopped calling and I don't know if he ever stopped throwing a rock and hiding his hand. Like this pastor,

# HERSTORY

IF YOU DON'T LEARN FROM HERSTORY, YOU'RE DESTINED TO REPEAT IT!

Sapphira and countless others, they failed to cross the separation line. When you cross the separation line, God can use you mightily. **Remember, gifts impress people but character impresses God.** Some people are still singing, preaching and teaching and God has fired them—they're not even on his payroll!

**And that ye put on the new man, which after God is created in righteousness and true holiness.**

Ephesians 4:24

**Behold thou desireth truth in the inward parts, and in the hidden parts shalt make me to know wisdom.**

Psalms 51:6

**Beware of false prophets, which come to you in sheep's clothing, but inwardly they are ravening wolves**

Matthew 7:15

**For there is no faithfulness in their mouth; their inward part is very wickedness; their throat is an open sepulchre; they flatter with their tongue**

Psalms 5:9

**SAPPHIRA**

## 2.) THE BOTTOM LINE:

In making important decisions, you must acknowledge God and ask him to give you divine wisdom. Find out the bottom line about the situation by discovering what God's Word says about it. Don't worry about the ABC or the 123 of it. Just know the Word and let God be true and every man a liar. I have listed scriptural references in the appendix of this book for the times that you need to see what God's Word says about a particular topic. If you allow God's Word to be the bottom line, you will not be tricked like Sapphira and Ananias. Living by God's Word and His wisdom will allow you the freedom of having nothing to **HIDE**, nothing to **LOSE** and nothing to **PROVE**.

## 3.) THE FINISH LINE:

The battle is not given to the swift or either the strong but to those who can hold out and endure until the end. Saphirra probably was faithful and truthful for a season but fainted in well doing. Galatians 6:9 lets the believer know that we will reap in due season if we faint not. Regardless of how tempting Satan's snares are, we must stay in line and refuse to break line. In other words, we must strive lawfully. We must be content with the pace that God is processing us and realize that we don't have to be the line leader all the time. Just hold fast because you may be next in line for your miracle breakthrough. When you cross the finish line and hear Him say, "Well done my good and faithful servant", it will be worth the struggle.

MY PERSONAL **HER**STORY PAGE

## *DISHONESTY*

> *"In making important decisions, you must acknowledge God and ask him to give you divine wisdom".*

**What important decisions are you facing? List them and ask God to help you to do his perfect will.**

_____
_____
_____
_____
_____
_____
_____
_____
_____

## *IN CONCLUSION*

Like the women in **HERSTORY**, everyone has a story to tell—a story that is rich, unique, and worthy of sharing. In the final analysis, as you and I stand before that Great White Throne, only the things done genuinely and sincerely for the sake of the kingdom will matter. It will not matter what others have to say about you, your family lineage, how much STUFF you've accumulated, how pretty you are, how successful you've been or what street you live on. The only thing that will matter is that you have gotten your business straight (like the woman at the well) and that your name is written in the Lamb's book of Life.

I don't propose to have ALL the answers, but have shared a few of the nuggets of wisdom that I have learned thus far during my own **HER**story. As time moves on, my story as well as your story, will continue to play until we hear His voice say, "WELL DONE MY GOOD AND FAITHFUL SERVANT." Our story is not over until He says it is over!

Until then, I challenge each of you to take time today to listen with a spiritual ear to the **HER**stories and HIStories of the people that you meet every day—while waiting in the dentist's office, when riding the bus, while talking on the phone, during your staff meeting-- -the possibilities are endless. Allow yourself to get off your high horse for a moment, pull off the mask, put pretty on pause, put sophisticated on hold, stop the pretense and dare to share a bit of yourself. Let somebody that's going through a rough time right now know that regardless of how turbulent the previous pages of their life **HER**story have been, God still has the last say so. As you witness to the people that God puts in your path, please allow yourself to be transparent before them while sharing pages from your own HERstory. Jesus can use your trials, tribulations, victories and successes to minister to the listener by reviving them and encouraging them to press on through whatever 'page' or 'chapter' of life that they are currently on. It is equally important that you allow the Holy Spirit to teach you to discern the lessons that you need to gleam from the HERstories that you hear because **'if you don't learn from HERstory, you're destined to repeat it'**

# **ANGER**

- The LORD is merciful and gracious, slow to anger, and plenteous in mercy. He will not always chide: neither will he keep his anger forever.

  Psalms 103:8-9

- He that is slow to wrath is of great understanding: but he that is hasty of spirit exalteth folly.

  Proverbs 14:29

- A soft answer turneth away wrath: but grievous words stir up anger.

  Proverbs 15:1

- But now ye also put off all these; anger, wrath, malice, blasphemy, filthy communication out of your mouth.

  Colossians 3:8

- Let all bitterness, and wrath, and anger, and clamour, and evil speaking, be put away from you, with all malice:

  Ephesians 4:31

# ASSURANCE / FOCUS

- And the work of righteousness shall be peace; and the effect of righteousness quietness and assurance forever.

     Isaiah 32:17

- For I the LORD thy God will hold thy right hand, saying unto thee, Fear not; I will help thee.

     Isaiah 41:13

- For the cause I also suffer these things: nevertheless I am not ashamed: for I know whom I have believed, and am persuaded that he is able to keep that which I have committed unto him against that day.

     2 Timothy 1:12

- My sheep hear my voice, and I know them, and they follow me: And I give unto them eternal life; and they shall never perish; neither shall any man pluck them out of my hand. My Father, which gave them me, is greater than all; and no man is able to pluck them out of my Father's hand.

     St. John 10:27-29

- Because he hath appointed a day, in the which he will judge the world in righteousness by that man whom he hath ordained; whereof he hath given assurance unto all men, in that he hath raised him from the dead.

Acts: 17:31

# ***ATONEMENT***

- But God commendeth his love toward us, in that, while we were yet sinners, Christ died for us. Much more then, being now justified by his blood, we shall be saved from wrath through him.

    Romans 5:8-9

- For all have sinned, and come short of the glory of God; Being justified freely by his grace through the redemption that is in Christ Jesus:Whom God hath set forth to be a propitiation through faith in his blood, to declare his righteousness for the remission of sins that are past, through the forbearance of God; To declare, I say, at this time his righteousness: that he might be just, and the justifier of him which believeth in Jesus.

    Romans 3:23-26

- For he hath made him to be sin for us, who knew no sin; that we might be made the righteousness of God in him.

    II Corinthians 5:21

And as they were eating, Jesus took bread, and blessed it, and brake it, and gave it to the disciples, and said, Take, eat; this is my body. And he took the cup, and gave thanks, and gave it to them, saying, Drink ye all of it; For this is my blood of the new testament, which is shed for many for the remission of sins.

Matthew 26:26-28

# ***BOLDNESS***

- And we have known and believed the love that God hath to us. God is love; and he that dwelleth in love dwelleth in God, and God in him. Herein is our love made perfect, that we may have **boldness** in the day of judgment: because as he is, so are we in this world.

    1 John 4:16-17

- For I know that this shall turn to my salvation through your prayer, and the supply of the Spirit of Jesus Christ, According to my earnest expectation and my hope, that in nothing I shall be ashamed, but that with all **boldness**, as always, so now also Christ shall be magnified in my body, whether it be by life, or by death. For to me to live is Christ, and to die is gain.

    Philippians 1:19-21

- Seeing then that we have a great high priest that is passed into the heavens, Jesus the Son of God, let us hold fast our profession. For we have not an high priest which cannot be touched with the feeling of our infirmities; but was in all points tempted like as we are, yet without sin. Let us therefore come **boldly** unto the throne of grace, that we may obtain mercy, and find grace to help in time of need.

Hebrews 4:14-16

# ***COURAGE***

- Be strong and of a good courage, fear not, nor be afraid of them: for the LORD thy God, he it is that doth go with thee; he will not fail thee, nor forsake thee.

    Deuteronomy 31:6

- It is God that girdeth me with strength, and maketh my way perfect. He maketh my feet like hinds' feet, and setteth me upon my high places.

    Psalms 18:32-33

- The LORD is my strength and my shield; my heart trusted in him, and I am helped: therefore my heart greatly rejoiceth; and with my song will I praise him.

    Psalms 28:7

- O, love the LORD, all ye his saints: for the LORD preserveth the faithful, and plentifully rewardeth the proud doer. Be of good **courage**, and he shall strengthen your heart, all ye that hope in the LORD.

    Psalms 31:23-24

- The LORD is my light and my salvation; whom shall I fear? the LORD is the strength of my life; of whom shall I be afraid? When the wicked, even mine enemies and my foes, came upon me to eat up my flesh, they stumbled and fell. Though an host should encamp against me, my heart shall not fear: though war should rise against me, in this will I be **confident**.

                              Psalms 27:1-3

# **DESPAIR**

- And the LORD, he it is that doth go before thee; he will be with thee, he will not fail thee, neither forsake thee: fear not, neither be dismayed.

    Deuteronomy 31:8

- We are troubled on every side, yet not distressed; we are perplexed, but not in despair; Persecuted, but not forsaken; cast down, but not destroyed; Always bearing about in the body the dying of the Lord Jesus, that the life also of Jesus might be made manifest in our body. For we which live are always delivered unto death for Jesus' sake, that the life also of Jesus might be made manifest in our mortal flesh.

    2 Corinthians 4:8-11

- The LORD is nigh unto them that are of a broken heart; and saveth such as be of a contrite spirit. Many are the afflictions of the righteous: but the LORD delivereth him out of them all.

    Psalms 34:18-19

- And hope maketh not ashamed; because the love of God is shed abroad in our hearts by the Holy Ghost which is given unto us.

  Romans 5:5

# *DISHONESTY*

- Lying lips are abomination to the LORD: but they that deal truly are his delight.

    Proverbs 12:22

- Finally, brethren, whatsoever things are true, whatsoever things are honest, whatsoever things are just, whatsoever things are pure, whatsoever things are lovely, whatsoever things are of good report; if there be any virtue, and if there be any praise, think on these things. Those things, which ye have both learned, and received, and heard, and seen in me, do: and the God of peace shall be with you.

    Philippians 4:8-9

- He that walketh uprightly walketh surely: but he that perverteth his ways shall be known.

    Proverbs 10:9

- These six things doth the LORD hate: yea, seven are an abomination unto him: A proud look, a lying tongue, and hands that shed innocent blood,...

    Proverbs 6:17-18

# *HOPE*

- For whatsoever things were written aforetime were written for our learning, that we through patience and comfort of the scriptures might have hope.

    Romans 15:4

- It is good that a man should both hope and quietly wait for the salvation of the LORD.

    Lamentations 3:26

- Be of good courage, and he shall strengthen your heart, all ye that hope in the LORD.

    Psalms 31:24

- Happy is he that hath the God of Jacob for his help, whose hope is in the LORD his God: Which made heaven, and earth, the sea, and all that therein is: which keepeth truth for ever:

    Psalms 146:5-6

- And hope maketh not ashamed; because the love of God is shed abroad in our hearts by the Holy Ghost which is given unto us.

    Romans 5:5

# **PERSEVERANCE**

- Blessed is the man that endureth temptation: for when he is tried, he shall receive the crown of life, which the Lord hath promised to them that love him.

    James 1:12

- And let us not be weary in well doing: for in due season we shall reap, if we faint not.

    Galatians 6:9

- And the Lord direct your hearts into the love of God, and into the patient waiting for Christ.

    2 Thessalonians 3:5

- To them who by patient continuance in well doing seek for glory and honour and immortality, eternal life.

    Romans 2:7

- But the God of all grace, who hath called us unto his eternal glory by Christ Jesus, after that ye have suffered a while, make you perfect, stablish, strengthen, settle you.

# ***WISDOM***

- Wisdom is the principal thing; therefore get wisdom: and with all thy getting get understanding. Exalt her, and she shall promote thee: she shall bring thee to honour, when thou dost embrace her.

    Proverbs 4:7-8

- For God giveth to a man that is good in his sight wisdom, and knowledge, and joy: but to the sinner he giveth travail, to gather and to heap up, that he may give to him that is good before God. This also is vanity and vexation of spirit.

    Ecclesiastes 2:26

- If any of you lack wisdom, let him ask of God, that giveth to all men liberally, and upbraideth not; and it shall be given him.

    James 1:5

- Wisdom strengtheneth the wise more than ten mighty men which are in the city.

    Ecclesiastes 7:19

- The fear of the LORD is the beginning of wisdom: a good understanding have all they that do his commandments: his praise endureth for ever.

     Psalms 111:10

- For the LORD giveth wisdom: out of his mouth cometh knowledge and understanding. He layeth up sound wisdom for the righteous: he is a buckler to them that walk uprightly.

     Proverbs 2:6-7

- But the wisdom that is from above is first pure, then peaceable, gentle, and easy to be intreated, full of mercy and good fruits, without partiality, and without hypocrisy.

     James 3:17

# **ENDORSEMENTS**

- "The book that you are holding in your hands was birthed through the spiritual womb of an anointed woman of God who has been appointed by Him to deliver this precious jewel to you. We are living in a time when there is a true crisis of meaning for many young women. The ten women of the Bible depicted in this book are role models and mentors that we can learn from. "Herstory" can become your story as you allow the Spirit of God to mentor you into wholeness. This is truly a book that can help unlock your destiny and purpose! Enjoy, and remember,

**As Long As There Is Breath In Your Body, There Is Hope(R)!"**

**Pastor Rosalind Tompkins-Whiteside, Founder of Mother in Crisis and Pastor of Turning Point International Church, Tallahassee, FL**

- "This book is an insightful journey that encourages, empowers and instructs women by showing them that as God's daughters they have powerful lessons to learn. By examining the lives of biblical women as well as the contemporary experiences of the author, one should emerge stronger and better equipped for productive Christian living. A very worthwhile reading experience for women who want to grow stronger in their Christian walk."

**Delores Y. Hudson, Avid Reader and Church School Teacher, Tallahassee, FL**

- "Pastor Davis has been used by God to produce an absolutely awesome, spellbinding reading that will certainly bless women from all walks of life. She has opened her heart to share some profound experiences that should capture the attention of many women and help them to release any bondage in their lives. This is obviously a best seller!"

**Pastor Rebecca Dickey, Pastor of Agape Covenant Fellowship Church and Founder of the Annual Women of Excellence Conference , Tallahassee, FL**